In Christ, you can BE
the best of who you
want to
BEE !

*What's Going On, Lord?*

Also by Thelma Wells
From Thomas Nelson Publishers


God Will Make a Way

# What's Going On, Lord?

Thelma Wells

THOMAS NELSON PUBLISHERS
Nashville

Published in Nashville, Tennessee, by Thomas Nelson, Inc.

Published in association with the literary agency of Alive Communications, 1465 Kelly Johnson Blvd., Suite 320, Colorado Springs, CO 80920.

Scripture quotations noted NKJV are from THE NEW KING JAMES VERSION. Copyright © 1979, 1980, 1982, Thomas Nelson, Inc.

Scripture quotations noted NASB are from the NEW AMERICAN STANDARD BIBLE ®. © Copyright The Lockman Foundation 1960, 1962, 1963, 1968, 1971, 1972, 1973, 1975, 1977. Used by permission.

Scripture quotations noted NIV are from the HOLY BIBLE: NEW INTERNATIONAL VERSION®. Copyright © 1973, 1978, 1984 by International Bible Society. Used by permission of Zondervan Publishing House. All rights reserved.

Scripture quotations noted KJV are from the KING JAMES VERSION.

**Library of Congress Cataloging-in-Publication Data**

Wells, Thelma, 1941–
    What's going on, Lord? / Thelma Wells.
        p.   cm.
    ISBN 0-7852-7030-2 (hc)
    1. God—Promises—Meditations.  2. Christian life—
Meditations.  I. Title.
BT180.P7W455   1999
231.7—dc21
                                                  98-39194
                                                  CIP

Printed in the United States of America.
2 3 4 5 6 — 04 03 02 01 00 99

*To the memory of my mother, Dorothy Nell Calhoun,
and in honor of my sister, Sarah Elizabeth Stinnett.
I appreciate you!*

# Contents

# *Acknowledgments*

$\mathscr{I}$ wish I could name all of the people who have helped me be successful during my fifty-seven years. The list would probably fill the lines on every page of a legal tablet. However, there are those who stand out.

My husband, George, and our children, Vikki, Lesa, and George Fitzgerald, are always the wind beneath my wings. God has given me a loving, supportive husband and three children who bring me joy, make me proud, brag on me, pray for me, listen to me, and give me advice. I thank You, God, for my family.

Patricia Mays, my administrative assistant, has said, "Thelma, I'm your armorbearer." At first, it sounded good to me but had little significance. I just did not understand what she meant. But once I learned that an armorbearer is one who works closely with you, understands your needs and works to help meet those needs, covers and runs interference for you when necessary, follows through on projects, keeps your schedule, helps you stay on track, outthinks you, travels with you, listens to your woes and celebrates your triumphs, prays with you and for you, and serves you in every appropriate way she can, I knew Pat was indeed my armorbearer. Pat prays for those who call our office for prayer, gives godly counsel to those who request it, manages the office, and still has time for her four children and seven grandchildren. And she also realizes that I am a frail human and that I occasionally make mistakes, but she appreciates me anyway. I praise God for Pat.

Brian Hampton, managing editor of Oliver-Nelson Books, is the wonderful young man who has worked with me on this book project. Thank you, Brian, for the time, energy, effort, and expertise you put into making this book possible.

Special recognition goes to Kathryn Yanni, my literary agent, Traci Mullins, my editor, and Vikki Wells, my publicist, who pushed me to get this published. To God be the glory!

*Introduction*

$\mathcal{O}$ne of the recurring questions asked in this book is, "What's going on, Lord?" As I looked back over my life, I heard myself ask more often than I'd like to admit, "Lord, what's the problem?" "What's this about, Lord?" "What's happening here, Father?" "What's up with this, God?" "What are You trying to say, Jesus?" "What's wrong?" "What have I done to deserve this?" "What are You trying to tell me, Lord?" "What?" "What?" "What?" It seems that these questions were the greater part of my vocabulary for the first fifty years of my life.

For every one of my *whats,* God had an answer. When I was asked to write my first book under an extremely tight schedule, I asked God, "What? How will I make it?" But He filled my mind and heart with the words He wanted. When He instructed me to quit my secure bank job to start my speaking business, I asked, "What? How will I survive?" But He prepared my husband to accept my decision and support me without regret. When my children were ready for college, but our funds were low, I asked God, "What's going on? How will we provide for them?" But Vikki was given four years of grants and work study with the help of a concerned school counselor; George Fitzgerald was trained for his profession by a jeweler who taught him everything he knew; and Lesa was given a full scholarship to cosmetology school by a loving church member. God had answered my *whats* even before I asked them. In other words, He had a plan.

The Lord declared, "I know the plans that I have for you, . . . plans for welfare and not for calamity to give you a future and a hope" (Jer. 29:11 NASB). I've learned from my experiences to rest in His peace until He reveals to me the answers to the *whats* of life.

Perhaps you have some *whats* in your life. You may be faced with a life-changing decision; concerned about a loved one; confused about your relationship with the Lord; disillusioned and disappointed with people; drained from the pressures of life; frustrated with your career; or reluctant to forgive yourself and others. Whether you are worried about the outcome of your circumstances, you have taken the situation into your own hands and messed it up, you are at the point of giving up, or you are patiently waiting on the Lord for an answer, this book is for you!

Whatever state of mind you're in, there are testimonies of hope in this book. When you read it, look for the faith-building strength in which we see the peace of God, the intercession of His Son, Jesus, and the power of the Holy Spirit bring light out of darkness; healing out of despair; cheer out of sadness; prosperity out of financial failure; strength out of weakness; forgiveness out of disappointment; truth out of misunderstood Scripture; and deliverance out of fear and anguish.

*What's Going On, Lord?* is written to strengthen people from all walks of life. Men, women, teenagers, urban, inner-city, or rural people; it doesn't matter. You may be employed or unemployed, homeless or not, saved or unsaved, strong or weak, overeducated or undereducated, physically challenged or well-bodied, it doesn't matter.

My earnest prayer is that you will be so convinced of God's personal relationship with you that your faith will increase, and you will have enough even during your *whats*. Paul urged, "Be anxious for [worry about] nothing, but in everything by prayer and supplication, with thanksgiving, let your requests be made known to God; and the peace of God, which surpasses all understanding, will guard your hearts and minds through Christ Jesus" (Phil. 4:6–7 NKJV).

Other verses offer encouragement:

The way of a fool is right in his own eyes,
But he who heeds counsel is wise. (Prov. 12:15 NKJV)

There is a way that seems right to a man,
But its end is the way of death.
Even in laughter the heart may sorrow,
And the end of mirth may be grief.
The backslider in heart will be filled with his
    own ways,
But a good man will be satisfied from above. (Prov.
    14:12–14 NKJV)

My God shall supply all your need according to His
riches in glory by Christ Jesus. (Phil. 4:19 NKJV)

Humble yourselves under the mighty hand of God,
that He may exalt you in due time, casting all your
care upon Him, for He cares for you. (1 Peter 5:6–7
NKJV)

Now to Him who is able to do exceedingly abundantly above all that we ask or think, according to the
power that works in us, to Him be glory in the church
by Christ Jesus to all generations, forever and ever.
Amen. (Eph. 3:20–21 NKJV)

For encouragement, read this book. Give one to a family member or friend. Your church library and bookstore need to have it available. Share it with your enemies. The worst thing that could happen to them is that they would be blessed. There is power in the written word.

A big hug to you because I love you!

Thelma

*What's Going On, Lord?*

# What's Going On, Lord?

## God Promises to Keep His Promises

$\mathscr{I}$ have the most beautiful granddaughter. Even her name, Alaya, is beautiful. I know every grandmother thinks that her grandchild is the best, brightest, and most blessed. So, yes, I'm typical. She is precious! But her birth really tested my faith. You see, I prayed for her even before her mother became pregnant.

While I was attending a Christian conference with my husband, daughter, and son-in-law, my spirit was led to pray for Lesa's unborn child. Of course, that shocked my daughter. She had no idea she was pregnant. She and her husband, Patrick, wanted a baby, but they had been trying to conceive for some time with no success. There I was praying for my grandchild while tears of hope and wonder streamed down Lesa's face.

A month later, Lesa and Patrick made the big

announcement. I was so happy. I knew that God had ordained this precious child and that he or she was the fulfillment of God's faithfulness to Lesa and Patrick and His revelation to me.

Lesa—five feet two inches and ninety-eight pounds—had a very easy pregnancy. The doctor ordered her to take two weeks of bed rest only near the end of her term, just to be safe. On April 29, 1996, she went into labor. I was out of town speaking when the call came. At first, everything seemed normal. Lesa commented that the baby felt as if it were turning flips inside her stomach, but everyone reasoned that the baby was just dropping. Then the baby's heart weakened and stopped momentarily, but the doctor was able to stabilize it and they thought everything was okay, that is, until Alaya was born.

She had turned blue—barely able to breathe with the umbilical cord wrapped twice around her neck. Her heartbeat was faltering. Her blood count was low. She was rushed to critical intensive care.

Not being there made it doubly hard for me to rest in the Lord. I wondered, *Heavenly Father, what's happening? Did You answer our prayers only to take the child back?* Mentally exhausted, my husband and I fell to our knees in prayer. While we were praying, I had a peace that I cannot explain. The Holy Spirit seemed to be assuring my spirit that Alaya would not die. Because my daughter had been in prayer and praise throughout her pregnancy, I believed God would honor her faithfulness in that hour of crisis.

Alaya got worse. The doctor said that she had reflux—the inability to retain food in the digestive tract. Although physical evidence gave little hope of her survival, I stood on the assurance God's Spirit had given me.

The first six days were the hardest. The doctor said the baby needed to be tested for signs of brain damage. The tests were inconclusive, but I knew she was fine. By day seven—the day of biblical completion—Alaya was released from the hospital. Today she is a healthy, beautiful two-year-old.

When you are distressed by uncertain situations—circumstances that appear to be hopeless—hold on to the fact that God is faithful. When you ask God for something and believe you have received a promise from Him regarding it, trust and do not doubt. God cannot lie (Heb. 6:18). He will keep His word to you.

# Prayer

*Father, Your faithfulness is to all generations. One thing You can't do is break a promise. Thank You for promising to keep Your promises. Give me the courage and patience to stand on Your Word even when circumstances make Your promises appear laughable. I acknowledge You as a God who does what He says He will do, and I praise You for Your steadfast care. Amen.*

## God's Word to You

No matter how many promises God has made, they are "Yes" in Christ. And so through him the "Amen" is spoken by us to the glory of God. Now it is God who makes both us and you stand firm in Christ. He anointed us, set his seal of ownership on us, and put his Spirit in our hearts as a deposit, guaranteeing what is to come. (2 Cor. 1:20–22 NIV)

## Affirmation

I will stand on God's promises to me regardless of the circumstances.

# A Calm in the Storm

## God Promises a Safeguard in the Midst of Turmoil

A while back, I talked on the phone to one of my dear friends. She was angry, fearful, exhausted, and wondering why God was not speaking to her and giving her directions as He had done in the past. She wanted me to tell her why. *I didn't know!* But as I prayed for wisdom and understanding, with the aid of the Holy Spirit, I was able to witness to her this way:

"Friend, when we become disappointed, angry, frustrated, and desperate, Satan can have a field day in our minds. He can load our minds with so much junk that we can't hear God or won't pay attention to the Holy Spirit when He's trying to talk to us. It doesn't matter how much we study the Bible, how long we pray, how constantly we praise God, Satan and his demons are waiting for one tiny port of entry into our minds to deceive us.

Satan's job is to confuse and frustrate us to the point of retaliation, rebellion, disobedience, and distrust in God. He is always out to disturb our peace of mind while we're waiting for the manifestation of God's promises to us."

We all have storms in our lives. Perhaps a loved one is on drugs, or we're experiencing physical or mental illness, financial difficulties, rejection, unemployment, painful conflict in a relationship, separation from a loved one by death or other circumstances, religious oppression, or legal trouble. I've certainly gone through some awful storms. In 1994, I asked God to give me a Scripture that could be my mainstay throughout that year. He always gives me more than enough. He gave me a Scripture that will sustain me every day of my life:

> Do not be anxious about anything, but in everything, by prayer and petition, with thanksgiving, present your requests to God. And the peace of God, which transcends all understanding, will guard your hearts and your minds in Christ Jesus. Finally, brothers, whatever is true, whatever is noble, whatever is right, whatever is pure, whatever is lovely, whatever is admirable—if anything is excellent or praiseworthy—think about such things. Whatever you have learned or received or heard from me, or seen in me—put it into practice. And the God of peace will be with you. (Phil. 4:6–9 NIV)

During the storms of our lives, we must not allow ourselves to concentrate on the frightening wind and waves around us. Remember what happened to Peter when he did that (Matt. 14:29–30)? Instead, we must direct our thoughts to the "whatevers" in the passage from Philippians. When we fix our minds on these things, we can experience God's peace and freedom from anxiety as we pass through our storms. Our hearts are guarded from becoming cynical and pessimistic.

When God gave me this Scripture, I had no idea I would need it as quickly as I did. That January, the southern and northeastern states experienced their heaviest snowfall in decades. I was scheduled to speak in Pennsylvania and Ohio on two consecutive days. Travel advisories were out all over the nation, and airport closings were commonplace.

Before leaving the airport in Dallas, I called my clients in both states to find out if the sessions were still scheduled. Both clients said, "Yes, come on." When I stopped over in the Cincinnati airport on my way to Philadelphia, I called my Pennsylvania client to find out if things were still a go. The client told me they thought it would be wise to cancel because the airport in Philadelphia had closed indefinitely and they weren't sure if I could make it or not. If I did get there, they couldn't guarantee that I'd be able to get out in time to make it back to Ohio to speak the next day. *Fine. That was a relief.* I quickly called the client in Ohio. "Yes," she said. "The meeting's on. We're expecting you."

By that time, the bag I checked in Dallas to go all the way to Philadelphia became a concern. I went to the baggage assistance counter of the airline to find out where my bag was. They told me it had been sent on to Philadelphia. *How could that be when no flights had left the airport since I'd arrived?* I needed my bags. And I was not going to Philadelphia; I was staying in Ohio.

"Help me retrieve my bag," I said, beginning to whine. "All my transparencies and clothes are in that bag. I need my bag!" Just as I started to panic, I remembered my Scripture, "Do not be anxious about anything." I stepped back from the counter, and with prayer and supplication I made my petition known to God. Suddenly I felt peace. My voice became milder; my attitude calmed; I smiled again. And as I stepped back up to the counter, the agent told me he had located my luggage. It was on the plane scheduled to go to Philadelphia. It could not be retrieved at the moment, but he would put in an urgent request to have it returned to the baggage counter. I should check back in about three hours. Meanwhile, he told me, the airline would put me up for the night in the hotel connected to the airport. He handed me some toiletries and a voucher for a meal, gave me directions to the hotel, and assured me that when my bag was returned, he would see to it that it was delivered to me. I walked away from that baggage counter with a sweet peace in my spirit, believing that everything would be all right. In about five hours, I received a telephone call from the baggage claim department telling me my luggage was there and it would be sent to me at the hotel.

While I'd been standing near the baggage counter repeating my Scripture to myself, I took a look at some other people standing there. Some were shouting, cursing, demanding, crying about the same situation I was in. I had almost been one of those people. Tears had begun to well up in my eyes. I had started to panic and take out my frustration on the agent. But thanks be to God, He had given me a Scripture that He knew I would need within a few days after receiving it.

I called my client yet a third time from Cincinnati before heading out. My rationale was, if they were going to cancel the engagement, I could return to Dallas from Cincinnati without losing too much time and energy. The client assured me that we were on for the program. So I rented a car at the airport and drove on icy roads to get to my hotel in Ohio.

I needed my Scripture again the following day when I finally arrived at my Ohio hotel near the site for my meeting. When I stepped up to the registration counter of the hotel, the clerk handed me a note that said, "Sorry you came. We've canceled the program." *Say what?* I nearly went ballistic! Fortunately I kept my mouth closed. My eyes told the desk clerk to give me a room in a hurry and to refrain from saying anything to me that might push me over the edge.

Sitting in my room, I tried to settle down. My Scripture came back to my mind, and I repeated it over and over until I felt calm. Once I relaxed, I was able to see the good in the situation. I could go back home the next day, earlier than I'd planned. I would get paid the same money without expending any more energy and time. I would, however, calmly explain to the client's meeting planner how inconsiderate it was to have me come and then cancel the program after I had confirmed with her three times. Because I prayed and recited the Scripture, my attitude was milder and more accepting than if I had not.

What a comfort to know that I don't have to go through airport delays, unwanted health reports, IRS audits, attitude adjustments, disagreements, or anything that constitutes a personal storm without God's always being in charge. That airport thing was just a tiny example of some of the other times that particular Scripture has helped me. I've quoted it to many people during their storms and have seen it quiet their spirits and calm their fears.

Remember my frustrated friend? Well, before we got off the telephone, she told me how much better she felt. Her circumstances were the same, but her hope was renewed and her faith increased by the Scripture God gave us all.

## Prayer

*Okay, Lord, I'm convinced. You really are in control while my storms are raging. You have the power to say, "Peace, be still." Master of everything, when I am struggling through the storms of life, please help me keep my mind on pure and righteous things. Help me realize that the storms cease more quickly when I trust in You. Thank You that I am able to speak peace to others because of Your peace in me. Amen.*

## God's Word to You

You will keep in perfect peace
    him whose mind is steadfast,
    because he trusts in you. (Isa. 26:3 NIV)

## Affirmation

In God is my place of calm during every storm.

# No More Monsters

## God Promises Peace When Fear Assaults Us

$\mathcal{I}$ loved my great-grandfather, Daddy Harrell. He lost his sight when I was young, and I gladly helped him get from place to place around the neighborhood. I was a brave little girl when I was leading him across the street. But at other times, I was a frightened little girl. When I closed my eyes at night, I would see skeletons and bogeymen. Horrible images of monsters and scary-looking faces would plague my mind. Sometimes I'd even see them when I had my eyes open; I imagined monsters or skeletons jumping out at me, chasing me around the house. That scary time in my life went on for months.

One day, a woman named Mrs. Mary Jackson came to the door of our upstairs back-alley apartment and looked through the glass panel on the front door. I went into hysterics. Her face looked like the monster that had been scaring me all those months. I remember screaming and crying as Granny tried to console me. I had been around Mrs. Jackson all my life; she lived across the street from us. Mrs. Jackson had given me many of the pretty clothes I wore. She helped pay for my piano lessons and school supplies. I knew she wouldn't harm me, but my mind was playing tricks on me. Mrs. Jackson looked like a monster!

Thank God for Daddy Harrell. He called to me from his favorite high-back, cane-bottom chair where he sat on the screened-in front porch and told me to lie down on the roll-away bed in the corner. Then he told me how to get rid of my nightmares and day visions of monsters and skeletons. I was to do three simple things:

1. Close my eyes.
2. Repeat the Lord's Prayer and the Twenty-third Psalm one after the other without stopping until I got relief.
3. Believe that God would make those monsters go away.

I trusted Daddy Harrell and believed everything he told me. I was scared, but I followed his instructions. The hardest thing was closing my eyes because I knew what happened almost every time I closed them.

I don't know how many times I repeated the prayer and the Scripture as I lay on that roll-away bed. I do know I began to feel at ease. I stopped crying. I stopped feeling frightened. When I finally opened my eyes, I looked up toward the sky and saw an awesome sight. More than forty years later, I can still see it in my mind's eye. The clouds had formed a huge figure of the head and shoulders of Jesus. He was looking upon me with pleasure, confirming to me that He had heard and answered my prayer. From that day to this, I have been free of the fear of monsters and skeletons.

When God delivered me from my nightmares, He also delivered me from the fear of being near thunder and lightning, traveling around the world alone, staying in a dark room, going out at night by myself, taking risks, and who knows what else. That's not to say I never feel frightened. Rodents are my worst fear. I hate rats! I also don't enjoy being tailgated. But being temporarily frightened doesn't compare to the horror of monsters taking over my mind.

God promises to deliver us from fear and torment, but that deliverance must be fueled by prayer, Scripture reading, faith in God, and obedience to Him. I have suggested this method of dealing with fear to my children, friends, and acquaintances because as simple as it may seem, it gets God's attention. He is the One who told us to humble ourselves as little children as we seek His face. The process Daddy Harrell instructed me in was a simple matter of taking my mind off the problem and concentrating on God. By recalling His Word and meditating on His character, I put my mind on Jesus, and He gave me perfect peace. Now when I walk through some valleys and dark places physically, emotionally, or spiritually, I don't have to fear. There are no more monsters.

## Prayer

*God, thank You for giving me a way to be delivered from my fear and trembling. When monsterlike situations come into my life, remind me that Your Word, prayer, and godly counsel can relieve me of all my apprehensions. What a mighty God You are! Amen.*

### God's Word to You

Yea, though I walk through the
    valley of the shadow of death,
I will fear no evil;
For you are with me;
Your rod and Your staff, they comfort me.
    (Ps. 23:4 NKJV)

### Affirmation

God delivers me from the "monsters" in my life and gives me peace of mind as I focus on Him.

# The Blessing in Receiving

## God Promises That If We Give, We Will Receive

---

*I* love surprises! I'm delighted every time someone gives me something unexpected. I feel blessed when nice things are done to or for me.

A blessing is an act of declaring or wishing God's favor and goodness upon someone. Most often, God blesses us directly or through other people when we are obedient to His command to bless others and give of ourselves for His glory.

I enjoy giving. I often ask the Holy Spirit to direct me to people to whom I can give money—people who may not even need it, but would be blessed by my thought and gesture of giving. God regularly leads me to people and makes clear to my spirit how much to give them. Sometimes it's not money, but other tangible and intangible gifts: an unexpected phone call, an encouraging note, a gift for no reason at all except to say, "I'm thinking of you." I can't count how many times I've thought of a person's name or seen his or her face in my mind's eye. I have learned to pray for people when they come to mind, or I get in touch with them. There's usually something going on in their lives that they need to share.

On May 21, 1997, I was in the Love Field Airport talking on a pay phone while waiting to board a Southwest flight to Lubbock. Two women and a little boy were sitting near me listening to almost every word that came out of my mouth. When I finished talking, the older woman stopped me and asked, "Are you the Woman of God?"

"Yes, I am. How are you?" (I knew she must be referring to my TV show called *A Woman of God*—unless I just had a particularly holy glow about me that day!)

The woman and her daughter said they were frequent viewers of my show and told me how much of a blessing the program was to them. After exchanging pleasant conversation, I left them and went to get a snack. When I returned to the waiting area, their arrivals had just come in from Lubbock. The younger woman called me over to her, took her sparkling fourteen-karat-gold bracelet off her arm, and fastened it on my wrist. She said that while I was walking away from them, the Lord told her to bless me with that gift.

I was shocked. I had never even seen those people before. The daughter said, "The diamonds aren't real, but I've enjoyed that bracelet. It's time for you to enjoy it. If you're ever prompted to give it to someone else, do so. It will bless her too." I continue to wear this bracelet with the spirit of love and respect in which it was given to me. It has truly blessed me. She and I now talk to each other by phone occasionally, and she always has an encouraging word for me. God has used one of my viewers to bless me unexpectedly as I've been obedient to do His work.

The speakers and staff of the New Life Women of Faith conferences have heard my bumblebee story so often that now they're on the lookout for bumblebee memorabilia. While I sit here writing this book, I can look around my sunroom and see bumblebee gifts that have been given to me from people all over the country. Elsewhere I have bumblebee soap, bath oil, dish towels, pot holders, light switch covers, flags, yard decorations— all given to me because people care and have been blessed by my ministry.

One of the most pleasant bumblebee gift surprises came my way in Pittsburgh, Pennsylvania, one Friday evening in August 1997. Barbara Johnson, best-selling author and speaker with whom I share the platform at the Women of Faith Joyful Journey conferences, had found some darling bumblebee house slippers in a shop in

Pittsburgh. Mary Graham, the mistress of ceremonies for the conference, followed Barbara's directions and surprised me with the gift of these precious bumblebee shoes before a crowd of 16,700 women. I wore them during the remainder of the evening, both onstage and at my book table. They continue to give me so much pleasure.

Many times, God surprises me with gifts only after I've given away tangible resources of my own. On a recent Sunday morning I visited a New Creation Fellowship Church where an evangelist had been ministering for several days. I had been praying during the week that God would clearly direct me to the person or organization He wanted me to give to next. While I was preparing to give my offering to the church that Sunday, my husband told me the amount he was writing his check for. It was a generous sum that ordinarily would have been sufficient for both of us. However, God spoke in my spirit again and told me to give the visiting evangelist $100 cash. I had it in my purse, but I didn't want to be broke. Giving away that $100 would have wiped out all my personal spending money. However, I had sold some books and had business funds, so I didn't really have an alibi for not parting with my cash. I dug around in my purse and came out with a $50 bill, thinking that should suffice. But again in my spirit I sensed God's voice: "What did I tell you, Thelma?" *Okay, God*. I reached back into my purse, grabbed the other $50 bill, and walked up to the evangelist and handed it to her. I felt good!

Less than a week later, I opened my mail, and there was a check for $100 from a dear friend who wanted me to have it for no particular reason. Wow! Once again, God was showing me that what I choose to do really does matter to Him, and He honors my obedience. The safest place in the whole wide world is the center of God's will.

When someone gives you a gift of a smile, friendly handshake, card, object, money, or whatever, how do you feel? I feel happy, delighted, humble, and sometimes embarrassed. But I always feel blessed. I feel that the giver is wishing God's favor and goodness upon me. That is the blessing in receiving.

## Prayer

*Father, I realize that people don't have to give, so when they do, I know You're in it. They're following Your prompting, obeying Your direction. Thank You for using us to bless one another, and for granting us the willingness to give without expecting anything in return. Help me to be open to Your claim on all my resources so that I can bless others in Your name. And thank You for all the surprises You have planned for me to receive. Amen.*

### God's Word to You

Give, and it will be given to you. A good measure, pressed down, shaken together and running over, will be poured into your lap. For with the measure you use, it will be measured to you. (Luke 6:38 NIV)

### Affirmation

As I give freely to others, I abundantly receive.

# God Does the Drawing

## God Promises to Confirm the Work of Our Hands

*I* was going about my morning routine at the office a few years ago when I had the idea to organize a women's retreat. I thought, *A women's retreat? I don't know anything about organizing a women's retreat. I don't have time to organize a women's retreat. I don't even* want *to organize a women's retreat. I can't conduct a women's retreat!*

But the notion kept invading my mind and tugging at my heart. When I spoke to my daughter Vikki and my assistant, Pat, about it, they thought it was a good idea. In fact, almost everything I suggest to them, concerning speaking and possibly making money, they think is a good idea.

Trying to figure out where to have it and how much to charge and other details started to consume my thoughts. Then I remembered to pray, "Lord, You know I don't know what I'm doing. Give me some people or resources to help me, please." He did.

I recalled that I had met a woman on an airplane not many months earlier. She had sent me a brochure of a company she worked for outside Flower Mound, Texas, called Circle R Ranch. I called her and scheduled an appointment to see the ranch. Then I thought of several energetic Christian women who were members of different churches in the Dallas–Fort Worth area and invited them to a meeting to create the format for a women's retreat. Over the weeks we prayed, fasted, and organized a retreat called Becoming a Woman of Excellence. (At the time I hadn't heard of Cynthia Heald's best-selling Bible study by the same name.)

We selected speakers, musicians, and volunteers, and one of the women who helped me plan offered to design and print the marketing brochures. They were not printed on slick, shiny paper, nor were they in vivid colors. I settled for black and white. After all, they were free!

Then came the first hitch. One speaker involved in the program saw the brochures and was disturbed because they did not look like the professional marketing pieces she and I were accustomed to. I think she was a little embarrassed to be promoted by such a low-budget piece. Because I respect her opinion very much, I agonized over it when she called her concern to my attention. I wondered if the other participants felt the same way but didn't want to hurt my feelings by telling me.

Confused about how to approach the situation, not knowing whether to discard the free brochures and spend money we really didn't have on more "classy" ones, I closed the door of my office and prayed, "Lord, I don't know what to do. Things have been going along so smoothly until now. What am I supposed to do about these brochures? Help me, Lord!"

I finished praying and started to go about what I was doing in the office. Suddenly the Holy Spirit seemed to confirm to me, "Mere paper does not draw people to God. *God* does the drawing!"

What a relief! The burden of trying to redo those brochures was taken away. Then my task was to tell the worried participant my decision and allow her to decide whether she wanted to take part in the retreat. I prayed again and asked God to give me wisdom in talking with her. He did.

I told her the truth. She had the choice of accepting or rejecting what I said. Since she is a gracious woman of God and a good friend, she said, "Okay, it's up to you, Thelma. It's your program. I'll be there." She made a tremendous contribution to the success of the retreat.

It's funny how we let little things that really don't

matter become problems. We need to keep in mind that whatever God ordains He sustains. I needed to remember that the idea of a retreat was not mine; it was God's. God already had the speakers, musicians, and volunteers picked out as well as the person who was to print the brochures. All I needed to do was to follow His plan. It was laid out perfectly and completely.

I'd been shortsighted when I'd asked God for forty women to attend the retreat. He drew 150 women from all over the state of Texas! On that day, women were healed from sicknesses and restored to emotional and spiritual health. Families were put back together, and participants found renewed confidence as women of God. We shared our dreams and spent private time with the Lord. Several women told me that things happened in their hearts that changed their lives for the better. I don't know all that happened, but God knows. He did the drawing.

Just think, I almost let a humble black-and-white brochure hinder the progress of what God had planned. I tried to talk myself out of doing what God had clearly told me to do. If I had, I would have aborted God's wonderful plans for many people to be healed and delivered that day.

Thank God that He is bigger than our hesitations, fears, and pride. When we obey His directions, He works miracles through us—even in spite of us. Hallelujah!

## Prayer

*Lord, I often ask You to guide me and reveal Your plans for me, but sometimes when You do, I foolishly try to get away with not doing what You tell me. (Shame on me.) Thank You for being patient and persistent with Your children. Thank You for trusting us enough to give us projects when You know we don't know how to do them, and for always being faithful to provide the mechanisms that bring about success. Thank You for being the kind and gentle Designer of our lives that You are. Keep us ever in Your will and in Your way. Amen.*

## God's Word to You

May the favor of the Lord our God rest upon us;
    establish the work of our hands for us—
    yes, establish the work of our hands. (Ps. 90:17 NIV)

## Affirmation

God's favor makes whatever I do for Him successful.

# *Divine Awakenings*

## God Promises to Communicate with Us

*I* often wonder why God wakes me up in the wee hours of the morning and puts ideas in my head. Is it because everybody else is asleep and He knows I won't be distracted? Is it because He knows that's the time I'm most receptive? It can't be because that's the time my name is called in His heavenly roll call. But invariably He'll wake me up between 3:00 and 5:00 A.M.

I wrote the credo for the Bumblebee Club, a group of supporters of my former television program, around 3:30 A.M.

I wrote the business plan for my company in the early-morning hours.

I pray for people before daybreak.

I meditate with God long before I do anything else.

Some of my most creative time is between 3:00 and

6:00 A.M. I'm awakened sometimes with groaning and travail from the bottom of my being. I've been warned of impending danger. I've known when some of my relatives have died.

One morning I had a dream that my husband's aunt, Essie V., was in a casket in the front of our church, but she was sitting straight up in the casket preaching. Immediately after that dream, God woke me up and confirmed in my spirit that she was dead. When my husband woke up later that morning, I told him what had happened. Almost as soon as I finished telling him, the telephone rang, and Aunt Doretha, Essie V.'s sister, told us she'd died that morning.

The dream about the casket had appeared to me before. Several weeks before Granny died, Mrs. Fay Pruitt, one of Granny's deceased friends, appeared to me as I saw Granny lying in a casket in front of the church. Mrs. Pruitt said, "Mrs. Harrell's coming and it won't be long." Immediately God woke me up. I knew Granny would die soon. My "death dreams" may sound morbid, but each time there was a calmness about the dreams that kept me from feeling frightened or upset.

I believe God talks to us. Have I ever heard God speak to me in an audible voice? No. Some people say that's how He talks to them. Other people say they feel Him inside their spirits.

God speaks to me in a variety of ways. Sometimes it's through dreams as I sleep and visions as I meditate. I can tell if it's God speaking to me because I can remember all the details of the dream or vision today as if I had just dreamed it.

Sometimes my left ear gets numb as He speaks in my mind.

Sometimes He speaks to me through Scripture.

Sometimes He speaks to me

- through the words of a song.
- through a reading or a sermon.
- through a quote or a prayer.
- through a word of advice or admonition.
- through the honesty of a child.
- from a billboard or a bumper sticker.
- through a conversation with a family member or friend.

But when He wakes me up in the wee hours of the morning, He has my complete and undivided attention.

When He speaks to me, He is never frightening.

He never tells me to do something that is harmful to myself or someone else.

He always tells me things that are in line with His Holy Word.

He does not always give me all the details.

His information is always correct.

When I follow His directions, I will make no mistakes.

He brings to pass everything He says.

I am amazed and humbled to realize that an awesome, omnipotent, sovereign God would want to communicate with me. But that's one of the reasons He created us: He wants us to have fellowship with Him. People have tried to explain how to hear the voice of God. In my opinion, nobody has been able to describe it fully. I believe God's sheep know the Shepherd's voice by faith.

If you want to hear whatever God has to say to you, simply ask. In the Lord's Prayer, these requests have to do with God's guidance in our lives:

- "Thy will be done in earth, as it is in heaven."
- "Lead us not into temptation, but deliver us from evil."

These requests alone open the door for God to personally communicate with us. Let us heed the voice of the Master.

## Prayer

*God, You are a Master at getting Your children's attention. Thank You for the unique ways You communicate with me. Please give me ears to clearly hear and do what You tell me. Many things would not be accomplished without Your guidance. Thank You for always being there to let me know which way to go. Amen.*

## God's Word to You

Whether you turn to the right or to the left, your ears will hear a voice behind you, saying, "This is the way; walk in it." (Isa. 30.21 NIV)

## Affirmation

God always communicates clearly to me when I listen.

# Anger Is Not a Virtue!

## God Promises to Transform Us into His Image

$\mathscr{I}$will never forget that October night when I deplaned at Washington National Airport on my way to Indian Head, Maryland, for a speaking engagement. The weather was pleasant outside, but my thoughts were tossing and turning on the inside. I'd been informed earlier in the day that in Indian Head, everything shut down in the early evening. The motel closed at ten o'clock. Out of the sympathy in her heart, a woman was going to stay there until midnight. If I didn't get there before midnight, I wouldn't have a place to stay. I'd be on my own.

The five o'clock flight from Houston to Washington, D.C., was delayed more than two hours. We sat on the runway in Houston all that time—time enough for me to start a whirlwind in my head. *What if I get to Indian Head and the woman is gone? What if I don't get there at all tonight? I have to speak at eight o'clock in the morning! What if my commute to Indian Head takes longer than I expect? What if the car rental counter is closed when I get there? What are my options?*

While my mind imagined various catastrophes, I developed a plan. *When I get off the plane, I will have my driver's license and confirmation number readily available for the car rental clerk. He or she will have empathy for me and will get me out of there quickly and efficiently.* I had it all figured out I thought!

I dashed off the plane and proceeded directly to the car rental counter, prepared with all the identification needed to make it a quick and easy transaction. My plan didn't work. The clerk had tunnel vision. I offered her my driver's license and confirmation number and asked her to enter them in the computer so the profile would give her instructions concerning the car. Her response to me was, "I need to see your credit card." I replied, "Yes, ma'am, I understand. However, if you will input my confirmation number, it will show you my profile, including my credit card information." She demanded, "I said, I need to see your credit card!" "Trust me," I answered. "If you will put the information into your computer, you will see what to do. This is an unusual situation, ma'am. I need to get to Indian Head, Maryland, before midnight." It was already 11:30 P.M. With an indignant tone of voice, the clerk exclaimed, "You must not have heard what I said. I said, *I need to see your credit card!*"

That did it! I lost my cool. I screeched, "Woman, you better put in my confirmation number if you know what's good for you! I'm going to Indian Head tonight if I have to take you with me." (I didn't realize until I left the counter that I was threatening to kidnap that woman.) I continued, "If you don't know what to do in unusual situations, ask somebody. Don't just tell me you need my credit card. If you would do what I ask, you would discover that the car rental is billed directly to the company I'm working for."

I continued my tirade until a young man came out of another area and asked what was going on. (He had heard me shouting, no doubt.) My gracious response to him was, "And who are *you*?" He told me he was the manager. Oh, boy, did I let him have it. I told him that he should be training people to understand and handle unusual situations, that as tired as travelers are at the end of a day, especially after waiting on a plane for more than two hours before takeoff, his clerks should be ready, willing, and able to give the most excellent customer service possible, which included listening to the customers!

He was so nice. He agreed with me. I had become so irate that I didn't even notice he'd taken my driver's license and confirmation number from me, put them into the computer, and presented me with car keys. He got my attention when he said the documents were in order, the car was ready, and he'd be happy to escort me to the vehicle.

Well, I wouldn't be outdone. With my hands on my hips and my eyebrows raised, I proclaimed angrily, "And anyway, do you know who I am? My name is Thelma Wells. I teach customer service all over the world." My eyes boring through the female clerk, I continued, "I teach people how *not* to get upset when they deal with people like *you*." I was downright ugly.

When I eventually got to Indian Head (much past midnight), there was no room at the inn. The only place to stay in the small town was at that no-name motel. I'd have to bunk down in my car for the night. About 2:00 A.M., a woman came out of one of the rooms to get a soft drink. I asked her for a blanket because it was cold. She declined. I also asked her if there was anyplace for me to get some rest. She told me to go to the first signal light and make a right. I did. I drove and drove, endlessly, it seemed, down dark, winding roads. It was so dark, I thought Big Foot would walk out of the forest any minute.

Just beyond a massive grove of trees I spotted a Shell service station sign. That was the most beautiful sign I had ever seen; it indicated that civilization was near. As I got to the intersection where the gas station was, I looked to my left and saw another beautiful sign: Motel 8. Swiftly I turned into the entrance, shuffled painfully to the office, and pounded on the door to get the desk clerk's attention. The woman was compassionate. Even though the motel was closed, she invited me in and comforted me while I told her about my ordeal. Thank God, I finally had a resting place if only for one hour. It seemed like the fastest hour in my sleep history.

Five A.M. came too soon. Time to arise and make that forty-five-minute trip from La Plata, Maryland, to Indian Head. I had to get back in time to stand in line with the construction workers and other contractors for a pass to enter the naval base where I was teaching.

Miraculously the day went well. Four o'clock came quickly, and I was off to Washington National Airport and the infamous car rental counter. I had more than an hour to think about the previous day and how I'd responded. I was not proud of myself. As a customer service and how-to-deal-with-difficult-people trainer, I had not done a good job of walking the talk. I had lost perspective on who I was and whose I was. I had allowed myself to act totally in the flesh.

When I'd asked the people at the car rental counter if they knew who I was, that question should have been

directed to me. *Thelma, do you know who you are? Do you know who you are representing everywhere you go? Do you think Christ would have acted as you did? Do you think the Lord is proud of your conduct? Do you have a repentant heart for the way you acted? Thelma, as a Christian, what are you going to do when you get back to that car rental counter?*

I walked up to the counter. The woman who provoked me was standing with her back to me facing the computer. I spoke to her. She looked around and saw me, then immediately turned back to face the computer. I spoke to her again in a pleading voice in an attempt to communicate, *I'm sorry for the way I acted*. Without turning to me, she shook her head. She would not let me apologize.

I've reflected on that situation for many years and have concluded that the clerk did not, in fact, "make" me mad. I responded to her based upon the storm that was raging within me. I felt totally at the clerk's mercy. When I felt I had no control, I fell apart and made a spectacle of myself.

As Christians, how often do we operate totally in the flesh and allow our jumbled thoughts and emotions to dictate our conduct? When I rushed into Washington National, I had already set the stage for that unsettling interaction. The what-ifs had me, and I wasn't going to be taken alive! So I worried and schemed. I don't remember asking God to take charge of the situation and have His way in it. I don't remember asking for protection and grace. I don't remember asking Him to give me peace in the middle of the storm.

The fact is, when we take charge of a situation without consulting the wisdom of God, we always make a mess of it. Relationships get convoluted, hearts get broken, unfair and unkind words are spoken, egos are crushed, waves of doubt trouble us, distrust creeps in, guilt takes up residence, and emotions go haywire. *Thangs ain't pretty.*

Think of the times you become angry or out of control. What's happening? Do you feel safe and secure? Do you feel competent and confident? Do you have faith that God is in perfect control of your life? I don't think so.

What do you think would happen in our lives if we would maintain an attitude of prayer in every single situation? What might have happened had I not attempted to manipulate the situation at the car rental desk? I believe I would have left there in time to make it to Indian Head before midnight. I know I would not have been hostile and belligerent. I would have been able to walk back up to that rental desk with a clear conscience. I certainly would have had more of a mind to thank God for His favor and protection on the trip.

Thank God, He never gives up on remaking us in His image! No matter how obnoxious our behavior is at times, He is willing to convict and correct us so that we can become more like Him.

## Prayer

*Lord, thank You for giving me all the ammunition I need to hold back the enemy of anger. Too often I take that innate emotion and use it against Your will in order to accomplish my own will. How often I stumble and make a mess! I take charge, talk out of turn, and refuse to listen to You as I should. Too often I already have my mind made up about how things should be. Your Word says that You are gracious and full of compassion, slow to anger, and of great mercy. By the power of the Holy Spirit, please conform me to Your image. Amen.*

## God's Word to You

And we, who with unveiled faces all reflect the Lord's glory, are being transformed into his likeness with ever-increasing glory, which comes from the Lord, who is the Spirit. (2 Cor. 3:18 NIV)

## Affirmation

Because of the Holy Spirit's transforming work within me, I will put aside my natural self-interest and behave more like Jesus.

# God's Miraculous Signs

## God Promises to Give Us Directions

*A* funny thing happened to me in Colorado Springs on August 18, 1997. I was there for an important meeting with people who help make me look good, my literary agent, Kathy, and my editor, Traci. The scenery was beautiful. The afternoon rain was gentle. The temperature, just right. Even though the tip of Pikes Peak was surrounded by pillows of white clouds and I could not see the whole mountain, just looking at that world wonder and seeing the foothills round about were spectacular. I had the pleasure of meeting new people, eating good food, and working in a comfortable, homey environment all afternoon. But I had no idea I'd be rewarded with the two extraordinary surprises I received near the end of the day.

Since I was a very young girl, I've believed that if you

want to know whether or not something's right for you, you need to ask God for a sign. I must have picked up the idea from hearing about God's giving signs of His favor or disfavor to people in the Bible.

For example, when I was fourteen years old, I asked God to give me a sign when I met the man I was going to marry. Sure, I was too young to be thinking about getting married, but people always told me I was old for my age. Anyway, I told God that when He wanted to show me who I was going to marry, I'd consider it a sign from Him if everything I did within one day was related to cleanliness. For instance, let me clean the house, change the sheets, shampoo my hair, take a bath, and do everything "clean" in one day. *Weird!* you say. Well, the sign made sense to me. You see, when I was a young girl, we had cold running water, but not hot running water. We had to boil water to wash clothes, and we did that only on Mondays. Most black folks didn't shampoo their hair more than every two weeks in 1956, and in Granny's house that was done on Saturdays. Other days of the week were designated for bathing, washing dishes, and so forth. To do all the "clean" things on one day would have been extremely unusual in our household.

I met my husband before I turned fifteen years old, even though we didn't marry until I was twenty. One Saturday God gave me the custom-made sign I'd asked for: I got up early and changed the linens on the bed and washed the clothes in the bathtub; I cleaned and mopped the kitchen; I dusted and swept the house; I raked the leaves off the grass and swept the porch; I went to the beauty shop for a shampoo; and I bathed that night. In Sunday school the next day I looked at George Wells for the first time. I said to myself, *I'm gonna marry dat boy!* I was convinced that this shy, quiet (I thought), handsome, skinny country boy was the husband God had assigned to me. All these years later, I'm still convinced.

Before I'd come to Colorado Springs to talk about the next book I was planning to write, I'd asked God for a confirming sign. I wasn't specific; I just asked Him to show me somehow, in a specific way I'd recognize, that I was following His perfect will. As Kathy drove me to the airport after our meeting that afternoon, the sky filled with the most gorgeous, awesome sight. Directly ahead of us were two rainbows. They looked to me like huge handles on the largest Easter basket in the universe. The aqua, yellow, orange, red, and purple bands were so brilliant they seemed to have spotlights illuminating them from behind.

I mentioned to Kathy that rainbows were significant in my life. I had asked God more than once to give me a rainbow during a very trying time to let me know that my personal storm was passing over and everything would work out all right. He'd shown me rainbows on three such occasions during the late 1980s. The double rainbow in Colorado Springs meant even more to me than anyone can imagine. I had never seen anything like that before, and I fully believe God was saying to me I was on the right track with the book I was writing. It *was* an assignment He had given me.

But that's not all that happened that August day. I flew home on American Airlines and was assigned seat number 5E. The person assigned to the seat by the window entered the plane with his wife. When I noticed that his wife was assigned to the row in front of us, I asked him if he wanted to sit with her. If so, I would gladly exchange seats with her. They were happy!

A young man sat beside me. I was so sleepy, I didn't really pay him any attention until we were well on our way to Dallas. He looked up at me from the book he was reading and got my attention. He said, "I know who you are." I thought, *He must have read my books or heard me speak. Finally, somebody's noticing me.* (Okay, maybe I was just a little full of myself for a moment.)

"Your name is Thelma Wells," he continued. "You were my first boss when I was seventeen years old. Do you remember me? My name is Randy Edwards."

*Randy? Randy Edwards?* I thought. *NorthPark Bank, maybe?*

Randy said, "I remember your face. But I really rec-
ognized you by your ring. I always thought that was the
prettiest ring. Mrs. Wells, you haven't changed a bit. You
are so special to me. Do you remember that you made me
go to school? I took banking classes because of you. Now
I have a degree in finance and work in many parts of the
world as a financial adviser in real estate."

My chest puffed up to a size sixty. I was a proud
puppy! *Just look at this young man,* I thought. *I had something to do with his success.* He didn't make my head any
smaller when he announced to his wife and her girlfriend,
loud enough for all of first class to hear, "Look, Honey,
this lady was my first boss and made me go to banking
school. Isn't this cool? My very first boss when I was seventeen!" Randy put the finishing touches on an already
unforgettable day.

If I had not gotten up and given that woman a seat
next to her husband, I might never have gotten to see
Randy. I took that as a sign that the good we do for others will come back to bless us. Randy sure blessed me!

According to *Strong's Concordance,* a *sign* is "an
unusual occurrence, transcending the common course of
nature." Some signs portend a remarkable event soon to
happen. Others are miracles and wonders by which God
authenticates the people sent by Him, or by which people
prove that the cause they are pleading is God's.

I believe God gives signs to all of us, even when we don't ask Him for them. But God doesn't always deliver the signs we ask for. When He doesn't, that, too, is a sign to heed. Often when I'm getting ready to make serious decisions, I ask for a specific sign to signal whether or not to go forward with what I think I want. For instance, when I was trying to make a decision about continuing my television show of one and a half years in 1997, I asked God for three signs within a certain time frame. I had to make my decision quickly. God didn't deliver any of the three things I asked Him for, and I took that as my sign to table the television show for whatever else God had in store for me. I had no idea what! I accepted God's non-delivery by faith. The time was right to end the show, and I did so on May 30, 1997. I accept all my signs by faith because God never lets me in on all the details about anything I'm contemplating.

Maybe you have asked God for a sign or for some evidence that He is working in your life. Many of the Bible characters took signs seriously, and I think we should too. Just read Deuteronomy 13:1–3; Joshua 4:4–7; Judges 6:17; 2 Kings 20:9; Isaiah 7:11; 38:7; and the other references to signs in the Old and New Testaments; and see how God used signs throughout the ages. It may seem silly to you to ask for a sign, but evidently God doesn't think it's so silly. He has used them for centuries.

Maybe you'd like to add this method to your other methods of communicating with God. You might be amazed at how He works when He actually delivers the sign you ask for!

---

### Prayer

*Father, You have used signs for generations to let us know what You want us to do. When we're making decisions or need something confirmed to us, You understand our humanness, and You often graciously meet our need for a tangible sign that we're headed in the right direction. When You don't give us an obvious sign, You give us Your peace instead. Thank You for being a God we can trust. Amen.*

---

### God's Word to You

"This is the LORD's sign to you that the LORD will do what he has promised: I will make the shadow cast by the sun go back the ten steps it has gone down on the stairway of Ahaz." So the sunlight went back the ten steps it had gone down. (Isa. 38:7–8 NIV)

## Affirmation

I am confident about my direction when I see the signs of God's favor and experience His peace.

# Did I Have to Get Burned to Listen?

## God Promises to Reveal Himself When We Are Still

We'd had a wonderful Fourth of July. Our children, their spouses, our grandchildren, and other relatives gathered at our home to eat fried shrimp, mashed potatoes, catfish, hush puppies, potato salad, lemonade, and ice cream. It was good (if I have to say so myself!).

After everyone had left, I had a serious craving for more shrimp. So I fixed some for George and me. We ate and reminisced about the day's activities. It had been a perfect day—talking, laughing, and enjoying our family. Now that I was alone with my honey, I rose to clean the kitchen. Then I could spend the rest of the evening with him.

The grease from the deep fryer was still hot. Because

I didn't want to wait until it cooled, I lifted the deep fryer and started pouring the grease into a plastic storage container. Well, you can imagine what happened next. The plastic container immediately started to melt, and I impulsively dropped the deep fryer. Hot grease splashed all over my right arm and hand.

*Oh! Mercy! I'm on fire! Don't panic! Don't panic! Get ice water! Get the medical book! Call 911! Do something!* My mind was in a whirlwind. My husband rushed me to the emergency room. After being treated, I learned that I had second- and third-degree burns.

I was not instructed to rest. And even if I had been, I probably would not have. I had too much to do. Yes, the pain was excruciating, but I had to speak at a conference the following day. And for months I had planned a trip with my daughter and grandson to the National Speakers Association annual convention the following week. I was scheduled to sing with an ensemble at the convention and participate on a panel. I had to be there. I had given my word.

By the time I arrived at the convention, I was exhausted. I was too tired to move. I tried to get out of bed but couldn't. My head was spinning, arm hurting, stomach rolling, body aching. I was sick! My immune system had shut down. I forced myself to keep my obligations (foolish, I know) because I wanted to keep my word. I figured that's what God would want (but did I really ask Him?).

I became more ill. The doctor at a local clinic informed me that I had a 104-degree temperature and gastritis. "Go home," he said. "Take these antibiotics. Drink plenty of water. Get some rest!" I finally did. I had no other choice.

Three days later at 3:19 in the morning, God woke me up. I sat up in bed just listening. I couldn't do much more. In the stillness I heard from God. In my spirit I knew He was telling me that my life was taking a new direction. Certain paths had come to an end and other paths were emerging. Finally He had my undivided attention. It had been too long since I had *really* stopped to ask Him what He would have me do. I'd been too busy forging my own agenda. Perhaps if I had not become sick and bedridden, I would not have sat still long enough to hear God speak to me so effectively. I'm sure He wanted to communicate with me earlier—on less-painful terms—but I was just too harried.

You don't have to learn the hard way as I did. You don't have to get burned to slow down and listen. You can stop and listen to God every day, quiet your spirit before Him, ask Him to communicate with You. God has plenty to say to you, but He requires your undivided attention. Psalm 46:10 tells us that we will *know* God and

His sovereignty when we are "still." Be still and know His will for you today.

---

## Prayer

*Father, You know all I have promised to do. What with home, church, social activities, and other responsibilities, I barely have time to breathe. Help me to slow down. Help me to just say no sometimes. I know You desire and deserve my time and my quiet dependence on Your guidance. I want to hear from You. Remind me to stop, listen, and wait on You each day. Amen.*

---

### God's Word to You

This is what the Sovereign LORD, the Holy One of Israel, says:
"In repentance and rest is your salvation,
    in quietness and trust is your strength,
    but you would have none of it. . . .
Yet the LORD longs to be gracious to you;
    he rises to show you compassion.
For the LORD is a God of justice.
    Blessed are all who wait for him!" (Isa. 30:15, 18 NIV)

## Affirmation

When I slow down and spend quality time with God, He reveals Himself to me.

# When God Says No

## God Promises to Show Us His Perfect Will

---

*F*or four years I was a part of the Business Incubation Center in Dallas and leased an office in that wing of the Bill J. Priest Center. Abruptly I was asked to leave because I had graduated from the business training program. *Well, what am I supposed to do now?* I huffed to myself.

My resourceful assistant and daughter found a wonderful building with ample office space in a prestigious area near downtown Dallas. To our amazement, the price was *right*! The lovely forty-two-year-old off-white brick two-story landmark on Fairmount seemed to have been an answer to two prayers. I wanted a convenient office location with enough working space for the machines and personnel. I had already planned in my mind the office I was going to build and how I was going to decorate it.

The desire of my heart was to be the proud owner of an office building with my name on the cornerstone and a sign in front with gold letters: THELMA WELLS AND ASSOCIATES. When we found this building, I abandoned my plan to build because I thought, *This is it!*

The building's owner lived upstairs in a lovely apartment with a beautiful picture window in the living room overlooking the front of the building. A large den, a modern kitchen, a pantry, two bedrooms, and two baths completed the apartment. There was even a deck in back. I could see myself having seminars and mini-retreats in that apartment. I daydreamed about that space all the time.

About a year after we moved into the office space downstairs, the owner died, and ultimately his daughter put the building up for sale. She did not list it because I had made it known to her that I wanted to buy the building. I loved the building. It was comfortable, convenient, and reasonably priced. I knew God wanted me to have this building. I had been praying to own it for a long time.

I was in for a rude awakening. I didn't know that people over fifty years of age, self-employed, without accounts receivable, were considered poor risks for a thirty-year mortgage. My friends in the banking industry all but told me to forget about it.

I huffed and puffed for days because nobody would finance the loan for the building. By the time I'd made my rounds of all the local bankers, the building owner's daughter had hired a Realtor, and people had started coming by to look at the property. I was cordial to them, but I still thought that somehow God was going to give me that building. After all, He knew how much I wanted it.

Time went on and nothing changed. Finally the Realtor purchased the building and moved into the lovely apartment upstairs that I thought was mine. *Hey! Wait a minute!*

At the time, I knew I'd be speaking for the New Life Women of Faith Joyful Journey conferences in several cities that fall, but I didn't know that within a month I'd become a permanent part of the group's plans for the future. But God knew. He had already planned for me to be debt-free and have no concerns about the maintenance of my own business property. The plans for my life did not include giving seminars and socials in that upstairs apartment. God knew I'd be on the road ministering to hurting women throughout these United States and the world. He knew that a building would be an added burden to my life. That was not His perfect will for me.

I love the promise in Psalm 37:23: "The steps of a good man [woman] are ordered by the LORD" (NKJV). My constant prayer for the past several years had been that God would close doors I didn't need to walk through and open doors I did need to walk through. I asked Him to keep me from wasting precious time. In His faithfulness to me, sometimes He said NO! to my passionate requests.

As I've studied what Scripture has to say about prayer, I've discovered these truths:

- *God answers all prayers.*
- Sometimes He answers them *immediately.*
- Sometimes He *delays.*
- Sometimes He says *no.*
- Sometimes His answer is a *surprise.*

God answers our prayers not according to our wishes, but according to His perfect will. Hallelujah!

Another thing I discovered is that when God says no, He gives us incomprehensible peace, which validates that His no is right on. As I've experienced His noes to me, once I've accepted His answer, He replaces the thing I thought I wanted with something even better. I'm glad He saved me from the headache of that building. The new owner is having to do costly repairs.

Several years ago I went through a similar process when I tried to buy a house. Nothing was working out the way I'd expected, and I got angry at the people and a little upset with God because I thought I knew what was best. In the end, I got far better than I was bargaining for: a much bigger house, better constructed, and half the cost of the one I thought I wanted.

Then there was the Mercedes-Benz I tried to get. It was just a status symbol that God knew I didn't need. My ego needed adjusting. So God fixed it! Once I was cured from that, He gave me a car I love with a monthly payment that doesn't make me sick every time I write the check.

Not being able to predict my future doesn't bother me anymore. God does such a great job! Why should I try to usurp His authority? I just pray and ask for what I think I want, then leave the rest to Him. It sure does relieve me of a lot of burdens when I let Him handle my life. After all, when I committed my life to Him, I told Him I wanted Him to be the Lord and Master over me and all He has entrusted to me. If I really meant it, I shouldn't have a problem letting Him control it.

The phrase "let go and let God" means a lot to me. The Thelma Wells version says, "Stop thinking you're running something when you ain't." God's got it all under control. Whew!

## Prayer

*I know You have my whole life under Your loving control, God. You know what I need, how much I need, and when to intervene and save me from things I have no business with. Sometimes I have personal objections to Your answers to my prayers, but to tell You the truth, Lord, I'm glad You take charge. Keep showing me Your skill in caring for my future. Keep teaching me to wait on You. Keep guiding me in Your plain paths. Thank You for showing me that when You say no, You also give me perfect peace. Amen.*

### God's Word to You

May the God of peace, who through the blood of the eternal covenant brought back from the dead our Lord Jesus, that great Shepherd of the sheep, equip you with everything good for doing his will, and may he work in us what is pleasing to him, through Jesus Christ, to whom be glory for ever and ever. Amen. (Heb. 13:20–21 NIV)

### Affirmation

God's noes are my opportunities to trust Him more.

# I Thought I Knew What I Was Doing

## God Promises to Increase Our Knowledge

$\mathcal{I}$don't like going to meetings. I found little value in attending the meetings of the organizations I used to affiliate with. So when Dennis McCuistion invited me to become a member of the North Texas Speakers Association (NTSA), I wasn't interested. He kept telling me that I was missing a great opportunity to improve my speaking business, but I was already a *successful* speaker, so what could NTSA offer me except a time commitment I didn't want?

Dennis and I met in the late 1970s when we were both teaching for the Dallas chapter of the American Institute of Banking, and we got better acquainted when we became members of the board of directors of the same banking organization. Since that time, Dennis and

I had become professional speakers. Dennis had gotten involved in the North Texas Speakers Association and the National Speakers Association (NSA) and realized the value of these organizations. Because my business was thriving, I really thought I knew everything there was to know about what I was doing.

Each time Dennis called to invite me to an NTSA meeting, I had an excuse to decline. But Dennis was his usual persistent self and wouldn't take no for an answer. Finally I agreed to attend one meeting to get him off my back.

That Saturday morning in 1986 was truly an eye-opening, humbling experience. I learned more about the business of speaking that morning than I could have learned in five years of owning the business. I became keenly aware of the fact that professional speaking was actually a business for me, no longer just a hobby. If I was to continue to succeed in this business, I'd better get organized, keep up-to-date documentation, and do a more professional job of contracting with my customers. I thought I was doing things very well. *Not!*

One other important fact stood out to me: the people in the organization were willing and happy to give one another information and guide one another in the right direction. I didn't know anyone but Dennis, yet they were willing to share information with me that could help me be a better professional. *Wow! What a giving group!* I thought. *I think I'm liking this.*

They announced that the National Speakers Association was sponsoring an upcoming workshop in San Antonio. I decided then and there to attend. The local chapter seemed too good to be true; perhaps the real scoop about this national organization would be revealed at the San Antonio meeting. When I went, I discovered the truth. The organization was indeed caring and giving. The workshops were full of information that I could use immediately. I was convinced: this was the organization for me!

In June I received a telephone call from the NSA informing me that I had been selected to present a show-case (an eight-minute keynote) at the NSA convention in Phoenix the following month. Me? Speak for the National Speakers Association? The caller assured me that she had the right person. Dennis's wife, Nikki, had sent my brochure and audiotape to the NSA without my knowledge. There was one little hitch: speakers are required to be members of the NSA, and I was not. "Ma'am, how much is the membership fee?" I asked the caller. She told me, and I promptly wrote the check and sent it by overnight mail. I would speak in front of the NSA in July.

The knowledge I gained from this group tremendously enhanced my professional speaking career. The day I presented my showcase, one of the owners of CareerTrack was in the audience. Within one month, I was traveling and teaching for CareerTrack, a national seminar company that contracts with professional speakers to teach business courses throughout the world. That period of time in my career propelled me to a more prominent position in the professional speaking arena. My visibility increased in industries I had not previously penetrated, and I gained credibility because of my association with professional speaking organizations. The peak of my NSA activities was when I was asked to deliver a keynote address in a general session at the Dallas national convention. It was the first time in the history of the NSA that a black woman was center stage before the entire convention. I would have missed the eventful occasion if I had not listened to Dennis and attended an NTSA meeting. I have learned to never say never. As determined as I was not to join another organization that meets regularly, by getting involved I estimate that I cut my learning curve for running my business by about five years.

God uses many methods to prepare us for the tasks He has assigned. Increasing our knowledge is not confined to the Bible; it is also confirmed by the Bible. Being open to learning from different sources is a sign of great wisdom.

## Prayer

*God, I don't know everything about anything. Thank You for both the obvious and the unexpected opportunities You give me to increase my knowledge so that I can serve You better. Help me to seek after knowledge as I seek after wisdom. Amen.*

## God's Word to You

I have filled him with the Spirit of God, in wisdom, in understanding, in knowledge, and in all manner of workmanship. (Ex. 31:3 NKJV)

## Affirmation

I embrace the opportunity to learn something new every day.

# It's Time to Go

## God Promises to Sustain Us as We Do His Will

Contemplating whether or not to quit my banking job and go into business for myself was a frightening dilemma. In 1972 I was hired at the Republic National Bank in Dallas as a proof operator. I reconciled big corporate accounts. Mothers were allowed to come to work at 10:00 A.M. and leave at 2:00 P.M., which fit well with my children's schedule. But I realized soon after starting the job that it was not my life's calling. I started praying that God would give me a job where I could feel much greater satisfaction, where I could move up and have some authority to use my innate leadership ability.

In 1974 I determined to get a better job, and NorthPark National Bank was my target. My husband and I banked there, it was near our home, and it was a

pretty place to be all day. I was going to work there! I
called the personnel director and asked him to meet me at
the door of the bank at closing time. With some objections that I did not accept, he reluctantly met me and
accepted my résumé. The challenge was on!

Several times a week I called to ask for an interview.
He kept telling me there were no jobs available. I kept
telling him there would be a job opening, and I wanted it.
Several weeks passed before the personnel director finally
called me in for a general interview (probably just to get
me off his back). Then there was yet another wait.
Impatiently and persistently I called the bank until one
day there was an opening in the New Accounts Department and I was invited in for a serious interview. On July
22, 1974, I became a member of the NorthPark National
Bank staff. Mind you, I knew absolutely nothing about
banking. Running a proof machine hadn't prepared me in
the least.

I moved up rapidly at NorthPark from the position of
new accounts clerk to customer service supervisor to
banking officer to assistant vice president. Within three
years I had also become an instructor for the American
Institute of Banking in Dallas, Fort Worth, Houston,
Austin, Chicago, and Minneapolis, as well as a trainer for
the Bank Administration Institutes throughout the state
of Texas. In some Texas banking circles I was described as

"the last word in new accounts." That's because an attorney and I had written a new accounts manual that outlined in detail all the legalities and methods of opening and maintaining new accounts documents in Texas. The manual was distributed throughout the state, and all the accolades I got in response to it and my teaching made it difficult for me to decide to take the plunge to leave the bank and become an entrepreneur.

While teaching banking classes in the late 1970s, I developed a short seminar about how people could become the best of whatever they wanted to be. Students in my classes began asking me to come to their banks, business organizations, club meetings, churches, and all sorts of other places to deliver that motivational speech. At the same time, people were inviting me to conduct training sessions on subjects I didn't know anything about. Someone would call and ask me if I taught telephone skills. "Of course!" I'd reply. I needed the business. I was willing to learn. Once a group was serious about hiring me to speak, I would spend hours, including many sleepless nights, to develop a seminar on that subject.

By 1982 the idea to quit my job and go into the professional speaking business full-time weighed heavily on my mind. I discussed my idea with my husband and asked for his blessing, but he did not believe it was God's timing.

There was no way I would go into business without my husband's full support. I considered his discomfort to be a clue about God's will, so I asked God to let my husband be in total agreement when the time was right. Two years later my family and I spent one of the most wonderful vacations of our lives in Montego Bay, Jamaica. As we were flying home from vacation, I knew in my heart that it would soon be time for me to confer with my husband again.

Going back to work was much more stressful than preparing for vacation. I sensed that something was about to change severely. My boss welcomed me back from vacation with a conversation concerning the direction he saw for the work I had done on the new accounts manual and other training products for the banking industry. He suggested that I allow the bank to market the products under the bank's name, and I would receive a small commission on what was sold. Because the material was not written just for my bank, but was being distributed throughout the state, that just didn't sound like a good business deal to me. The passion for going into business for myself was getting stronger! So was the fear of leaving my "secure" position.

When lunchtime came, I collected my purse, several sharpened pencils, and a legal-size yellow writing pad, and I headed for Wyatt's Cafeteria in the NorthPark Mall.

"Lord, give me wisdom," I prayed. "I've got to really think about what I'm going to do." I had read somewhere that Dr. Viktor Frankl developed a method of dealing with fear called paradoxical intention. I recalled the method and used it to help determine what the next step in my decision process should be. This is what I did:

1. *Wrote down the situation.* I needed to determine whether or not to leave my banking job and start a full-time professional speaking business.
2. *Wrote down all the advantages and disadvantages.* I made a list of all the pros and cons I could think of for leaving my job and for going into business for myself.
3. *Determined the worst case scenario.* What was the worst thing I could expect to happen if I left the bank and started my own business?
4. *Asked, "What difference will it make?"* As I reviewed all my pros and cons, I asked myself how important they would be in the next one to five years.

The last question helped me decide that it was indeed time to ask my husband again for his support. How would I ever know whether or not I could make it in business if I never tried? At that point I penned a new definition of failure. To me, *failure* is never trying to do what is in your heart. Psalm 37 reminds us that when we live for God and want to be in His perfect will, He places desires in our hearts that are designed to help us carry out His will more fully. I was convinced He had placed the desire for my own business deep within my heart.

Excited but nervous, I waited for the right time to approach my husband with my thoughts. Once I told him about the offer my boss had made, George felt the same sinking feeling about it I had. His emphatic response was, "It's time to go out on your own. If you don't do it now, you're going to do it sooner or later. Go for it!" *Okay!*

Then I got really scared. My dream was becoming reality. It was time to tell my boss that instead of allowing the bank to exploit my handiwork, I was going to quit. Writing my resignation wasn't easy. After working at the bank for more than ten years, I had status, authority, a paycheck, insurance, and other perks and benefits. *What in the world was I doing?* But the passion of my heart to be a professional speaker spoke louder than my fear. I'd known for some time that what I really wanted out of life was to travel globally, extracting diamonds out of people's dust. All I wanted was to help people be better people. It was time to go!

Just to make sure, I sought the opinion of someone who loved the Lord, lived for Him, and would give me her honest perspective on my thinking process. I called George's aunt, Doretha Cashaw, and told her I had something urgent to talk with her about. She came by my house that evening, and I told her of my decision to resign from the bank and start my speaking business. She asked me if I had talked to the Lord and my husband about it. When I answered yes, she gave the best philosophical/theological thesis of anyone I had paid attention to in a long time. She said, "If God said do it, you do it. What God ordains, He sustains. Step on out there in faith, Baby. Everything we do is in faith whether we know it or not. What do you have to lose if you're doing it for God and He gets the glory?"

Much to my boss's dismay, I resigned effective August 17, 1984. Three days later I walked back into that bank as a training consultant and got my very first large contract to continue training for the bank until the end of the year. God financed my business without my having to borrow a single penny. What a mighty God we serve!

You may be facing a frightening decision in some area of your life. Be assured that God knows all about the situation. He also has a solution for you. Ask Him for wisdom. Ask Him to show you what He wants you to do. Trust Him to know what He's doing. I have discovered that God places ideas in our minds for a reason: He has a plan for each of us, and He provides the time, resources, and people to help us reach our heartfelt goals. If you are obedient to God's Word and are committed to fulfilling His plans for your life, you can face the human fears of decision making with the assurance that God is in control of the situation.

These past years as a full-time professional speaker have not been without trial and error, loss and aggravation, heartache and tears. But the good times far outweigh the bad times. God knew what He was doing.

## Prayer

*Lord, I'm glad You know everything. You know what I should be doing and when I should do it. You know my purpose in life and how my experiences build wisdom and faith for future challenges. When I become fearful of the future, please remind me that You are sufficient in everything. You are in control. It's great to realize that I'm not out here making decisions alone. Your Holy Spirit is guiding me all the time. May that blessed assurance make me act boldly, even when I feel afraid. Amen.*

 *It's Time to Go*

## God's Word to You

For I the LORD thy God will hold thy right hand, saying unto thee, Fear not; I will help thee. (Isa. 41:13 KJV)

## Affirmation

Even when I am afraid, I can confidently follow the path God has laid out for me.

# The Thirty-Day Book

## God Promises to Make the Impossible Possible

The telephone rang at my office about 10:00 A.M. several years ago with a request I thought was impossible to fulfill. An executive from the National Speakers Association (NSA) asked me to have my book at the Dallas convention site within a month. I was to be the keynote speaker for a general session of the NSA, and all keynote speakers were expected to be published. I wasn't aware of that when I accepted the pioneering opportunity to be the first black woman to speak for a general session.

"My book?" I sputtered. "Did you say my book? What book? I'm supposed to have a book, am I?"

My daughter Vikki was listening to me stutter and sputter and told me to give the telephone to her. After discussing the nonbook as if it existed, she declared, "Oh, yes, Thelma's book will be delivered by that date. You can depend on that."

*What in the world had she done?* She had just put my reputation on the line by implying that I had a book, and she was crazy enough to tell the NSA executive it would be there within thirty days! I felt sick to my stomach. I wanted to throw up. But Vikki reminded me that the speaking invitation was an honor. Was I going to blow it by not having a book? According to Vikki, *not on your life.*

My question was, "How in the name of all that's right can I get a book written, published, and delivered by the deadline?" I saw no possible way of accomplishing what Vikki had just promised. Well, Miss Vikki had it all figured out. "Listen," she instructed me, "you've got the outline. You know what you're talking about. You've got the stories to go with it. While you're traveling, write. Fax what you've written back to me and leave the rest to me. Okay? Do you understand? Do it!"

Like a good mother, I did it—nervously. While I was writing and faxing, Vikki was doing research, collecting a network of proofreaders, getting endorsements, hiring an illustrator, and lining up a book printer. My self-published thirty-day book would be a masterpiece or bust!

Fortunately we remembered to stop and pray. We asked God to give us the wisdom, knowledge, people, printer, stamina, creativity, and everything we needed to make the impossible project possible. We realized that without Him orchestrating the details, we were like a ship without a sail. We couldn't be smart enough, innovative enough, or clever enough to do it all without the aid of the Holy Spirit.

Need I say that everything worked together perfectly? The book was called *Capture Your Audience Through Storytelling,* and Vikki believed it would be a best-seller. On the thirtieth day following the startling telephone call, she drove to Austin to pick up the impossible book that had been finished, and she delivered 1,800 copies to the convention site before the deadline. The day I spoke, I sold almost all the copies. Since that time, the book has been purchased by thousands of people and organizations and is still in as much demand today as it was that day in 1993.[1]

Perhaps you are facing impossibilities in your life— things you know you can't do on your own. You don't know how. (Vikki and I didn't know how.) You don't know who to ask for help. (We didn't know who to ask.) You don't know where to go. (We didn't know where to go.) But God did! If you have projects and ideas that have lingered dormant in your mind because you've assumed that finishing or pursuing them is beyond your grasp, think again. Don't underestimate God's ability to bring "impossible" things to pass. When He places an idea in your head, trust that He has provided all it will take to bring it to fruition.

Often our biggest problem is not lack of skill or resourcefulness or time; it's lack of faith. We don't *believe* things can happen. But God specializes in things that seem impossible. He can do what no other can do! Depend on Him to guide and direct you. He wants to. Trust Him!

## Prayer

*Father, I really need to trust You when I have ideas or demands that seem impossible to fulfill. I see You working things out all the time, and yet I resist asking You to make the impossible possible. Your power and patience amaze me, Lord! Thank You for showing me that all I have to do is call on You for assistance, and You gladly give it. Nothing is impossible with You. Amen.*

## God's Word to You

For with God nothing shall be impossible. (Luke 1:37 KJV)

## Affirmation

I bring all my challenges to God, who specializes in accomplishing things that seem impossible.

# God Sent Us to College

## God Promises to Make a Way Out of No Way

When I was a girl, my family was poor and had no means of saving money for my college education. Granny, Daddy Lawrence, and Uncle Jim made sure I had the necessities and some of the luxuries of life, so I didn't know we were poor or just how poor we were until I got old enough to read the poverty indexes.

Oh, how I wanted to go to college! After the secretarial school I tried to enroll in threw me out because of the color of my skin, Granny and I became more and more determined to find a way for me to go to college. Granny talked to her employer, Mrs. Mary Less, who was a wealthy white woman living in University Park in Dallas. Granny was one of her maids. Mrs. Less asked me to come to her house to discuss my college aspirations. When I did, she offered to send me to North Texas State

University. She would pay my tuition and buy my books on the condition that I kept my grades above a C. If I got married before graduation, my husband would have to cover my bills.

Was I excited or what? Mrs. Less kept her end of the bargain. Daddy Lawrence gave me five dollars a month for the Laundromat, and Granny sent me "care packages." My roommates and I cooked at our off-campus home, and we walked to school, so there was no need of transportation money. God *did* make a way.

When my husband and I got married on April 1, 1961, Mrs. Less's obligation became null and void. Thank God, my husband realized what he was going to have to do to send me to college. He did. I graduated from North Texas State University in August 1963 after getting married, changing my major from business administration to secondary education, having one child, and conceiving my second one.

My daughter Vikki wanted to attend the University of Texas at Austin. When she applied to college, our income was high, but so was our debt. I went to Austin during student orientation and waited for almost an entire week to meet with the financial counselor assigned to Vikki. Once I had a chance to talk with her, she told me that Vikki's loan had been approved for $269. *Say what? Two hundred sixty-nine dollars for four years? I don't think so!* I showed her our income statement and all the bills we owed. I needed to prove to her that even though we made money, we were living from one paycheck to the next. (That's nothing to be proud of, but in 1979 I didn't have the same money management skills I have now.)

Miss Smothers tried to prove to me via computer that Vikki's financial aid application had already been processed and that there was nothing else that could be done about the results. But after she'd spent about twenty minutes attempting to pull up Vikki's record on the screen with no success, I had her attention. Miss Smothers consented to reenter our financial statistics, and when she ran the new data through the computer, she was able to match Vikki up with more academic scholarships and work-study than my daughter needed for the entire four years! God knew what He had in store for Vikki's future and saw to it that she got her education, regardless of the financial limitations of her parents. God sent Vikki to college.

My younger daughter, Lesa, never wanted to go to a four-year college. Her goal was to become a hairstylist and own her own business. To be a successful businessperson, she decided she needed to take business courses at Mountain View Community College in Dallas. By the time Lesa was ready to start community college, we were financially prepared to send her. (She is seven years younger than Vikki.) However, we didn't have to pay for Lesa's education, either. The Branch/Roland Scholarship Committee at St. John Missionary Baptist Church gave her a scholarship to Mountain View, and Mrs. Ella Mae Rollins paid for her beauty school education. Now Lesa is the owner of her own beauty salon where six operators help people look beautiful every week. Praise God!

Little George had the good fortune of working in a jewelry store when he was in high school. The master jeweler in that store took George under his wing and taught him all he knew about jewelry repair and design. George also attended the Gemological Institute of America to hone his skills. He now works for one of the largest jewelry companies in America.

You may have some dreams and goals that seem unreachable. Sometimes we can't see how we can possibly accomplish our objectives. But I'm here to tell you that if you keep the faith and trust in the Lord, He will open doors that you have no idea exist. What Granny said is true: whatever you want bad enough that's within the perfect will of God, the Lord will make a way for it to come to pass. You better believe it!

## Prayer

*Lord God, You are awesome! You are the God of computers, education, money, and all good things that come our way. Thank You for making a way when it seems there is no way. Thank You for placing people in my life who care about my future and are willing to be used by You to accomplish Your will for my life. You are truly an omnipotent God! Help me to hold on to the truth that You have everything under Your control; You will work it out. Amen.*

## God's Word to You

Not that we are competent in ourselves to claim anything for ourselves, but our competence comes from God. (2 Cor. 3:5 NIV)

## Affirmation

I trust God to accomplish His plans for me.

# The Doctors Had Given Up

## God Promises His Healing Power

May of 1995 was a traumatic time in the life of my friend Ed. She was riddled with oppression, guilt, shame, depression, anguish, and self-destroying thoughts. Overcome by those plagues, she shot herself in the head to end it all.

I got the call in Austin, Texas, and did not believe my ears. "What? Kill herself? She has two beautiful daughters, a good husband. She is well educated, beautiful to look at, a Christian person. How could she do something like that?"

During recent Sunday school classes, I'd noticed that Ed often posed questions about how God can forgive heinous sins, yet not relieve us from remembering them. Occasionally she was moody and distant and behaved in ways I did not understand. Once I asked her if anything was wrong, and she mentioned a few somewhat trivial problems, everyday struggles we all have. I took her at her word and did not ask God for discernment or try harder to get to the heart of what was going on inside my friend. Neither I nor Ed's other friends knew what was really happening. Later we talked about not seeing the signs of her depression and despair and how bad we felt about that.

I returned to Dallas and went to Parkland Hospital's Intensive Care Unit to see my friend. She was not expected to live. The medical team had given up. I looked at Ed's swollen, dark, mutilated head and face. I was told that a part of her brain had to be removed to reduce the swelling and inflammation. The prognosis was either death or life in a vegetative state.

But I believed God had a plan to do more than just keep Ed breathing. My friend Debra Young had spoken to me by phone before I got to Parkland and told me to speak only life and read life-giving, healing Scriptures because Debra believed with all her heart that Ed would live. "Do not believe the report of the doctors!" Debra urged. "Together, let's trust God for a miracle!"

One of the members of the medical team was my friend. He pulled me aside and begged me to stop people from praying for Ed's recovery. Our praying was giving false hope to her family, he said. It was disturbing and a waste of time. My reply to him was, "If God can make a brain, He can restore a brain." We *would* keep praying and reading healing Scriptures.

I must confess, my faith got weak during those first several weeks, and I started to doubt that Ed would recover. I thought, *Well, maybe it's not God's will to heal her.* Isn't it funny how Satan can infiltrate your mind even when you know you serve a healing Jesus?

Within a few days, Ed started moving her leg and responding to questions by squeezing our hands. Within a few weeks the swelling was gone. Her eyes were following us. She began to smile. Ed said she was glad she had failed in her suicide attempt. Through the weeks she came to realize she had much to live for.

I asked her why she did it. "At the time, I thought that was the only way out of my misery," she said. "Now I know that if I just could have *talked* to someone about all the guilt and anger I was carrying around inside me from childhood, I wouldn't have felt so hopeless. I'm sorry I put everybody through this. I didn't know there were so many people who cared about me."

Progressively she gained strength. Her vital signs became normal. She was sitting up and receiving visitors. Soon we were taking her riding in her wheelchair. She was moved to a rehabilitation center. After a few months she went home to her family, and within one year she went back to her job. She was not the same as she was before the shooting because she still had some motor slowness and did not drive her car. But members of the medical team at Parkland Hospital are now convinced (whether they admit it or not) that nothing less than a miracle of God restored my friend to physical health.

Ed is now in a support group where she gets ongoing counseling, and most of her immediate family members are in counseling as well. Each time I see Ed, I see a different person. More and more, she is smiling, happy, content, and whole.

At one of my seminars a year after the incident, Ed told her story to the audience. She wanted people to know that there are many options for solving their problems; suicide is not one of them. She was glad she'd finally faced her problems and was getting professional help to handle them. Most of all, she was glad that God had forgiven all of her past sins and that her family was healing from what she had done.

God has promised that He will heal our sicknesses: "Is any one of you sick? He should call the elders of the church to pray over him and anoint him with oil in the name of the Lord. And the prayer offered in faith will make the sick person well; the Lord will raise him up. If he has sinned, he will be forgiven. Therefore confess your sins to each other and pray for each other so that you may be healed. The prayer of a righteous man is powerful and effective" (James 5:14–16 NIV).

The problem with believing that God wants to heal people lies in the fact that not everybody is healed. The apostle Paul had a thorn (pain, suffering, or physical infirmity) in his flesh. He pleaded with God three times to remove it. God refused. But God gave him sufficient grace and power to live with his infirmity.

God certainly doesn't always heal in the ways we expect. Because He is sovereign, He has many options. I've seen Him heal instantly; through medical procedures and processes; through death (the ultimate, most revered healing for a Christian, in my opinion). Just because we doubt, just because we haven't experienced healing, or just because we think miracles are not for this modern day doesn't stop God from doing what He promised in whatever way He chooses.

*The Full Life Study Bible* lists ten things that can hinder healing:[1]

1. Unconfessed sin
2. Demonic oppression or bondage
3. Acute anxiety
4. Past disappointments that undermine present faith
5. People

6. Unbiblical teaching
7. Failure of the elders to pray the prayer of faith
8. Failure of the church to seek and obtain the gifts of miracles and healing as God intended
9. Unbelief
10. Self-centered behavior

Sometimes the reason for the persistence of physical affliction in godly people is not readily apparent. In still other instances, God chooses to take His beloved saints to heaven during an illness. Until God makes His perfect will known, we can take some steps when praying and seeking His healing for our bodies:

1. Be sure we are in a right relationship with God and others.
2. Seek the presence of Jesus in our lives, for He will give us the faith we need.
3. Saturate our lives with God's Word.
4. Examine our lives to see what changes God may desire to work in us.
5. Call for the prayers of the elders of the church with the anointing of oil as well as the prayers of family members and friends.
6. Attend a service where a person with a respected healing ministry is present.

7. Expect a miracle—trust in Christ's power.

8. Rejoice if healing comes immediately; rejoice if it does not.

9. Know that God's delays in answering prayers are not necessarily denials of those requests. Sometimes God has a larger purpose in mind that, when realized, results in His greater glory and is good for us.

10. Realize that if we are committed Christians, God will never forget or forsake us! He loves us too much to leave us.

I can say with all confidence that we serve a healing and delivering Jesus. My friend Ed is a living testimony. But when the God who made us and knows all about us chooses not to heal us, I believe He always gives us the strength to handle our reality, just as He did for Paul. The fact that some Christians experience healing and others do not does not mean that God thinks higher of some than others; I believe that He knows whom to trust with certain circumstances. He knew that Paul would be a shining example of how God can sustain His children in the midst of sickness and suffering.

Perhaps you have been pleading for healing for yourself or someone else and you're not seeing any results. Don't become frustrated and disappointed with God. Ask

Him to put peace in your spirit and contentment in your soul as you persevere. Continue to pray and ask others to pray with you. Above all, praise God for the strength to make it through the situation. Maybe God is trying to tell you that He trusts you too. You can be a model for other people going through similar things.

If you see other people get healed, don't begrudge them their blessing. Be glad for them! God has a different plan for each of us, and He loves us all perfectly.

## Prayer

*Dear Lord, You're there when we're sick. You're there when we're well. You hear when we pray. You forgive when we doubt. Sometimes my intellect gets in the way of my constant faith. I wonder if You will, sometimes even if You can, heal as You said. Yet even in my fog, You assure me You are still in complete control. Please give me the grace to persevere in faith, no matter what my circumstances. Amen.*

## God's Word to You

Surely he took up our infirmities
    and carried our sorrows. . . .
The punishment that brought us peace was upon him,
    and by his wounds we are healed. (Isa. 53:4–5 NIV)

---

## Affirmation

I serve a healing Lord.

# He'll Die at Fifty-Nine

## God Promises to Lead Us into All Truth

 

*I* had never heard of tarot cards until one of my secretaries of years past brought them to my office. She introduced them as a fun way to look into the future or to entertain at a party. I thought, *I like to have fun. I'm curious. Why not?* I felt a little uneasy, but I didn't want to be a party pooper. Just like everybody else, I wanted to know the future. So I let Giselle conduct several readings for me. They always yielded positive predictions. She told me about career promotions, financial success, traveling abroad, and business ventures I would have. That was good! I liked being reassured of my success.

But one day Giselle looked alarmed as she read my cards. "I hate to tell you this," she hesitated, "but you will marry twice. Your husband will die at age fifty-nine."

"Stop!" I shouted. "I don't want to hear any more." I became sad, frightened, and suspicious of the game. *How can she predict when someone will die?* I thought. *Only God knows that.* Still, I was scared. My husband, George, was forty-six, and we had already been married nineteen years. You know the song "Wind Beneath My Wings"? Well, George is my wind. He encourages me, directs me, trusts me, loves me, supports me, listens to me, confirms me, and gives me peace in the midst of life's challenges. I cannot imagine life without him, and I don't want to.

Over the next thirteen years I begged God, "Please spare George's life!" When George turned fifty-nine, I pleaded, "Please forgive me for my foolishness, Lord! Please let my husband live." I was scared and ashamed, but I didn't share my thoughts with anyone.

As I turned to God for direction, His Word reassured me that the Holy Spirit would guide me into all truth. I don't need any tarot cards to tell me what's in store for the future. The apostle Peter taught that God Himself gives His people messages He wants communicated; human beings can't prophesy on their own:

> For prophecy never had its origin in the will of man, but men spoke from God as they were carried along by the Holy Spirit. But there were also false prophets among the people, just as there will be false teachers

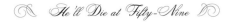 

among you. They will secretly introduce destructive
heresies, even denying the sovereign Lord who bought
them—bringing swift destruction on themselves. Many
will follow their shameful ways and will bring the way
of truth into disrepute. In their greed these teach-
ers will exploit you with stories they have made up.
(2 Peter 1:21–2:3 NIV)

I came to believe that my secretary was a false
prophet, and I knew God had forgiven me for my foolishness in listening to her "prophecies." I began to feel a
peace about George.

He is sixty-three years old now, healthy, and quite
cute! God is so merciful to us. Even when we stray from
His teachings and experiment with demonic devices, His
blood covers us. I could have become immersed in the
psychic, mystical, magical culture. Satan makes it so
appealing, especially when we are uncertain about our
future. But the Bible calls fortune-telling and tarot cards
abominations to God (Deut. 18:9–12). He does not want
our reliance to be on anything but Him.

When you have a need to know your future, turn to
God. Ask for wisdom and guidance. He knows what is in
store for you, and He will reassure you that He is in control of your destiny. He has promised to direct your path
when you trust in Him.

## Prayer

*Jesus, keep me from relying on the words of others for guidance. Yes, there are Christian friends who will give me godly advice, but my total reliance must be on You. Thank You for forgiving me when I foolishly pursue the world's ways of gaining knowledge. You are the God of all truth, so I will trust in You with all my heart to direct my future. Amen.*

## God's Word to You

But when he, the Spirit of truth, comes, he will guide you into all truth. He will not speak on his own; he will speak only what he hears, and he will tell you what is yet to come. (John 16:13 NIV)

## Affirmation

God holds my future in His hand and will direct me by His Spirit of truth within.

# My Child Would Never Do That!

## God Promises Never to Forsake Our Children

One of the most devastating truths for parents, especially Christian parents, is that their children can and do stray from their teachings. Many kids get involved in drugs, sex, pornography, witchcraft, or gangs; become school dropouts; abuse their parents; defy authority; and behave in many other heartbreaking ways.

I remember, during the early days of my teaching career, going to a friend's house to inform her that her son was breaking into the vending machines at school. She was furious with me. "My child would never do that!" she told me emphatically. "We give him everything he needs. You'd better stop lying about him." I took her cue and stopped telling her anything about her child, but

I continued to watch the situation. While his mother remained in her denial, the child got more and more into a life of crime. To this day he's in trouble with the law.

There came a time in my life when shocking information was presented to me concerning children I had tried to influence. I discovered that they were experimenting with drugs. At first I blamed their peers. Then I pointed the finger back at the parents and eventually at God. After all, didn't His Word say, "Train a child in the way he should go, and when he is old he will not turn from it" (Prov. 22:6 NIV)? That's a principle that many Christians refer to without fully understanding its meaning. What was God doing?

As I pondered the meaning of this Scripture, I wondered if I was missing something. I studied the word *train* and discovered that it means "to dedicate." Parents must commit themselves to training their children in the ways of God. We must attempt to create in our children a desire and appetite to experience God for themselves. We must dedicate our children to God and dedicate ourselves to the stewardship of our children that God has entrusted us with. But we must remember that the world, with its evil charm and cunning influence, is used to persuading children to sin. Choices are offered; wrong choices often are made. Paul wrote, "For all have sinned and fall short of the glory of God" (Rom. 3:23 NKJV).

So what's the deal? I went back and read the proverb carefully. I realized it didn't promise that our children would *never* stray from the path we set them on; it said, "When he is *old* he will not turn from it." As the years have gone by, I've seen that principle fulfilled. For a long time, Satan confused these children's minds and bodies, but not their souls. Even while they strayed, they never forgot their parents' biblical teachings. Scripture still rang in their ears. Respect for Jesus remained deeply embedded in their hearts. I watched a long progression of some from the hostile, headstrong, immature kids to the determined, funny, happy, God-loving adults they are today.

God's Word is true. And when we feed it to our children, it will not return to Him void. Isaiah 55:11 (NIV) declares,

> So is my word that goes out from my mouth:
>   It will not return to me empty,
> but will accomplish what I desire
>   and achieve the purpose for which I sent it.

Our God has promised never to leave us or forsake us (Deut. 31:8). Children do stray. But God doesn't abandon them. We may hold fast to His promise to remain faithful to them.

# Prayer

*Lord, sometimes I get frustrated and frightened when You let children continue in their temptations and sins. I need strength to continue praying, that they will not permanently depart from the teaching that has been instilled in them. Thank You for the encouragement that You will never leave them or forsake them. Help me as a parent to train my children in Your ways, and then give me the faith to trust You to bring the work You've begun in them to completion. Amen.*

## God's Word to You

The LORD himself goes before you and will be with you; he will never leave you nor forsake you. Do not be afraid; do not be discouraged. (Deut. 31:8 NIV)

## Affirmation

I rejoice in God's faithfulness to my children and trust what He is doing in their lives.

# *Why Do You Complain?*

## God Promises to Deliver Us from Fear

 

 

 

 

                                     Elle was one of the most reliable, conscientious, hardworking people in my bookkeeping department at the bank. She was always on time, didn't take advantage of breaks, took little or no sick leave. She was a loyal employee. There was only one big thing wrong: she whined, complained, and behaved like a victim all the time. There was not a day that she didn't come to my office to tell me what some other employee was or was not doing. She felt she was the only person working and carrying the load in the department. Everyone else was talking on the telephone, going to the rest room too much, chatting with other employees, coming back late from lunch, or doing something she considered worth reporting. I wondered how she could do all the work she was doing and keep tabs on everybody else.

She had made such a habit of coming into my office to complain that every time I saw her coming, my nose started to itch. I was not comfortable with the state of affairs!

When I became a supervisor, I had absolutely no supervisory training. I didn't have an educated clue about what I was supposed to do about an employee like Elle. I just had to rely on common sense. One weekend, after being perplexed all week about what I needed to do to stop her complaints, I came up with a brilliant idea. I created a form that listed every employee's name, and I left space for Elle to enter information about what the other people in the department were doing. I would make Elle the monitor of the bookkeeping department. Job description: snoop on everybody and write it down. Report back to me with documentation of everyone's behavior.

Monday came and Elle didn't disappoint me. When she came into my office, I was ready for her. I was actually excited to see her. I asked her to be seated and told her how happy I was that she had taken it upon herself to look out for the department's well-being. I showed her the form I had created with all her colleagues' names and specific columns to record the various behaviors that she was to monitor. I told her, "Elle, I'm making you the official watcher of the department. These people are not pulling their load, and we need to nip this in the bud. I want you to document what they're doing. If they go to the rest room and stay too long, write it down. If you think they're on a personal phone call, write it down. If you see them clocking in on more than one time card, write it down. If they go to lunch early or return late, write that down. If they talk ugly to the customers, write that down. I want you to record every wrong thing they do and report back to me in one month. When you bring the documentation to me, bring the people with you too. We'll stop this!"

Elle was horrified. She responded with an emphatic no. She did not want to cause a problem; she just thought I wanted to know what was going on in the department. She could not bring "those people" into my office. She wasn't that brave! Her refusal didn't surprise me at all. She didn't want to confront her colleagues face-to-face. She wanted to come in and complain to me. I told Elle that if she could not comply with what I asked, she should never come in again complaining and whining without documentation and the person in tow.

I nipped that thing in the bud, all right. Elle never whined to me again. But the situation still perplexed me. I wondered why Elle thought it was so important to tattle on other people. I knew she was much older than some of her colleagues and she had been on the job for many years. She had no academic skills, just the skills she had developed on the job. She was her sole support. She was a loner and lived a lonely life, with only her cat to keep her company. Her son and daughter visited sometimes, but she didn't seem to have much of a social life. I was concerned about her.

Later I was promoted to supervisor of the personal banking division of the bank. Having worked first as a new accounts clerk and then as a bookkeeping supervisor, I had learned a lot about the needs of both areas. One of the most poorly managed areas in the bank was the signature cards and other account documents. Those documents were used by several departments, but no one was in charge of holding people accountable for taking them out of the files and returning them. More often than not, someone would come to look for a file, and nobody would know where it was. The situation needed attention. And I had the perfect solution!

I made Elle the official guardian of the signature cards and resolution files. She was free to rearrange the files in a more functional way so that she could get to them easily. She developed a form like a library rental card to check the documents in and out to employees. On the form were the name and department of the person, the time of day, the due date, and any other information Elle thought pertinent.

I have never seen anyone perk up and look as needed

and important as Elle did. What she'd really wanted all along was to be assured that her job was secure. I discovered that all her whining and complaining was a smoke screen for what was really happening inside. Elle was scared of being replaced by someone who was younger or had more education. By creating that job for Elle, I gave her what she needed. She was able to regain her confidence and be proud of the job she was doing without the interference of all "those other people." When it was time for Elle to retire, she did so with dignity and security.

Sometimes people we think are chronic whiners, complainers, or victims may be sending us a message. They may be trying to tell us that they're afraid and need assurance and support. The experience with Elle has helped me be less critical of people who exhibit similar behavior. I have learned that there is a reason why people act the way they do.

Just as Elle was acting out of fear, so do many Christians. Experts believe that most people have four basic fears:

1. The fear of failure
2. The fear of rejection
3. The fear of risk or loss
4. The fear of success

I'm sure everybody has had all these fears at one time or another. That's only human. However, the Bible has something to say about how Christians should respond to fear: "The fear of man bringeth a snare: but whoso putteth his trust in the LORD shall be safe" (Prov. 29:25 KJV). Fear can be a reliable deterrent to an unsafe or harmful situation, or it can paralyze our efforts to move from one place to another in our lives.

By admitting to the fear and allowing myself to analyze *why* I'm afraid, I usually discover I don't know how to do something or how it will turn out if I do. It's good for me to talk about it to another Christian who I know will offer me godly counsel. The Bible is full of passages that console me and give me strength as I walk through that period of fear. And then, either I tackle the situation with all the ammunition possible, or I delegate it to someone with more expertise. I try to remember that when I am obedient to God and work to satisfy His will, I can claim Isaiah 54:4 (KJV): "Fear not; for thou shalt not be ashamed: neither be thou confounded." Elle was not shamed. Through concern and observation, using common sense, I was able to understand her situation and do something about it.

Whatever your fear, God has someone or something in place to help you. Whining, complaining, and behaving like a victim are not viable ways to resolve your fears.

Such behavior only makes them worse because each time you talk about your fears without resolving them, you are rehearing them instead of dispelling them. Problems become more and more intense and ingrained as you constantly discuss them.

You can change your behavior. Think about the things that cause you the most fear. Ask yourself why you're so afraid. Talk about the fear to someone you trust. Pray to God to help you overcome it. Study what the Bible says about fear. Sing praises to God or listen to music that gives praise to God. Willingly release the fear. Watch God work in your life to replace fear with confidence!

## Prayer

*Father, I am so glad I can call You Father, because good fathers listen to their children's fears and do something to help them overcome them. There are so many places in the Bible where You tell us not to fear, for You are our refuge. You take good pleasure in protecting us. How grateful I am that when I am afraid, You never shame me, but You deliver me and set my feet upon a rock. Amen.*

## God's Word to You

For God hath not given us the spirit of fear; but of power, and of love, and of a sound mind. (2 Tim. 1:7 KJV)

---

## Affirmation

I never have to fear because God is taking care of me.

# Who Likes Criticism?

## God Promises Growth from Wise Counsel

*I* don't know of anyone who really enjoys being criticized. But whether we like it or not, criticism is what all of us get at one time or another. Sometimes constructive criticism is easier to take than ruthless faultfinding, but criticism is criticism. It's rarely pleasant.

One day I was preparing to go into a seminar when a woman I didn't know walked up to me and said bluntly, "Your hair sure is an ugly color." (Admittedly I kept cosmetic companies in business because at that time I colored my hair every six weeks. That particular week my hair was Sparkling Sherry.)

I responded to this lovely woman this way: "Thank you. I'm glad you were paying attention to my hair. I color it every six weeks. The next time I do, I'll remember what you said. It's always great to have an unbiased opinion."

She was speechless. I had taken her power away! Perhaps she thought she could make me feel bad, but she was wrong. The fact is, I had looked in the mirror that morning and left home pleased with the way I looked (hair included). I had a choice when she said those critical words to me. I could have responded with hostility and anger. I could have ignored her. I could have used my sense of humor. I chose the latter. I turned a potentially negative statement into a positive response.

Some of the best growing I've ever done has been the result of criticism, whether constructive or destructive. In my opinion, constructive criticism occurs when someone addresses the situation instead of the person, for example: "Betty, I have some questions about this report because it doesn't seem to be complete. Can you tell me what to look for or how it can be corrected?" Destructive criticism tears down the person instead of addressing the situation appropriately: "Betty, you made a mistake on this report. Can't you ever complete a task? Get this corrected and give it back to me."

One of the most powerful people in my early corporate career was an officer at a bank where I worked. She could correct me and criticize me, yet make me happy. I remember several times I goofed up an account. She would come quietly to my desk and ask to speak to me in private. Her comments generally ran along these lines: "Thelma, you are learning this business quickly. I'm proud of your progress. We do have a situation that needs your attention. Mrs. Whoever called and said her checks were ordered incorrectly. I see that your name is on the order. Can you please find out what happened, who was affected by what happened, and how we can prevent this from happening again? You can get back to me before leaving today if you get this information. Thank you. I know you'll take care of it for us."

Man, did I feel important! I thought, *She trusts me to get this information to her. Boy, I'm good.* As I would go through the process of getting the information, I would learn more and more about the ways each department depended on the others, how to be more observant, and so forth. The officer was teaching me all the time she was criticizing me.

Even when we don't enjoy being criticized, we must admit we learn some things about ourselves that we'd have never known had we not been criticized. Over the years, I've learned techniques for taking the sting out of receiving criticism so I can benefit from it. This is what helps me:

- I consider the source. Is the person criticizing me genuinely interested in my well-being?

- I consider the circumstances. Am I clear on the circumstances that caused the criticism?
- If the criticism is appropriate and accurate, I agree with it. Who is going to argue with me when I'm agreeing with her?
- If I wish to have more explanation concerning the situation, I ask for it. Getting complete information about why someone said something or what's wrong with something is another way to learn.
- If I don't agree but don't want to have a damaged relationship, I evade the issue by using noncommittal words such as *maybe, I guess, it seems, possibly, you think?, perhaps, I'll try,* and phrases that don't cost me anything but make the person feel that I'm agreeing with him.

Maybe one reason I've been married as long as I have is that I use that last technique with my husband! Sometimes when he's fussing at me about something, I say, "Honey, perhaps you're right. Maybe I need to listen to you more. The next time this happens, I'll try to pay more attention. Thank you for calling this to my attention." I don't admit to anything, but what I say sure makes him feel good.

On the other hand, criticism can be very wise counsel when accepted with an open mind. The book of

Proverbs talks a lot about it. Read Proverbs 8:14; 12:15; 15:22; 19:20; 20:5; and 27:9. Remember, when you're faced with criticism, you have a choice. You can get hostile and defensive, or you can heed King Solomon's words and follow his advice. Basically he was saying, "A wise person takes criticism and extracts from it what can help her grow. A foolish person denounces criticism and stunts his growth."

Be wise. Grow from criticism.

## Prayer

*Lord, You use some of the most unique methods to help me become what You want me to be. Criticism does not make me feel good, who wants to hear what's wrong about him or her? But wise counsel is so important to You that the wisest man who ever lived took a lot of time to write about it, under Your direction. Frankly, God, I can always use feedback to help me become a more excellent servant for You. Help me to take it in the right spirit and use it wisely. Amen.*

## God's Word to You

The way of a fool is right in his own eyes,
But a wise man is he who listens to counsel. (Prov.
12:15 NASB)

---

## Affirmation

I listen to criticism with an open mind and take from
it what can help me grow.

# A Recovering Perfectionist

## God Promises Completeness Through Him

We never talked about perfection in my house when I was growing up. I think it was just a given. I remember having to get up every morning and make my bed perfectly. I had to wash and dry the dishes and stack them perfectly in the cabinets. Straightening up the linen closet, arranging the towels perfectly, was another chore. I was expected to iron my dresses perfectly and bleach my clothes so that the whites were perfectly white.

At school, I had to have perfect attendance. My homework had to be flawless, within the lines, and complete. My lunch pail was packed carefully so that none of the foods would touch the others and spoil the taste. The pail was aired out each afternoon so that it would be perfectly fresh for the next day.

At church, I was expected to be a nice, quiet, intelligent girl. I learned my Bible verses and hymns and recited and sang perfectly. The one time I forgot my lines was the worst day of my life up to that point.

Uncle Jim and Aunt Allene took me to fine restaurants in our neighborhood and taught me table manners and etiquette so that I'd have perfect social graces. I designed and directed all the elements of my wedding, including staying up all night before the big day to make sure it would be perfect. When I look at my wedding pictures now, I marvel at the beauty of the sanctuary and the standing-room-only crowd that attended. But I wonder why somebody didn't notice that my hoop slip was longer than the length of my dress!

After marriage, I attempted to be a perfect wife and mother. I had no idea that wives and mothers had to do so much stuff. I was the one who had to make the stripes in the towels hang straight, pull the sheets taut before making the bed, and keep the kitchen spick-and-span. For years, I tried to live up to my standards. I didn't know they were unreasonable until my body started to rebel.

I started having headaches, passing out, being depressed to the point of being hospitalized. My doctor and the team of psychiatrists ran all kinds of tests and uncovered my problem: I was trying to be perfect. I was trying to live up to what I thought were everybody's expectations of me. I wanted to please everyone and do perfectly what everyone asked me to do.

My doctor demanded that changes be made in my thinking patterns and activities. He talked with my husband about the problem. Soon I learned for the first time that all the things I compulsively focused on were not nearly as important to George as I imagined. He never said he wanted me to do everything perfectly; I just assumed he did.

Changing behavior is not an easy thing to do, so the doctor suggested I take baby steps. I was to resist the urge to make my bed the instant my feet hit the floor. I was to practice not cleaning off the table the minute we were finished with a meal. The first time I left the bed unmade, I felt guilty and untidy. Thirty minutes were all I could take! But that was a start. It's been nearly thirty years since I stopped trying to be perfect. It's been about twenty years since I could detect a real difference in my thinking and let go of my self-imposed guilt for not doing everything "right."

I have coined my own definition of *perfectionism:* "a neurotic, destructive syndrome designed to make you feel guilty when you don't do what you think everybody else in the world wants you to do." From personal experience I have found that true perfectionists are pains in the neck. They never live up to their standards, but neither does anyone else. When they make a mistake, it follows them around like a dark cloud.

Someone gave me this anonymous writing one day, which contrasts self-limiting perfectionism with the self-liberating pursuit of excellence:

Perfection is being right.
Excellence is willing to be wrong.
Perfection is fear.
Excellence is taking a risk.
Perfection is anger and frustration.
Excellence is powerful.
Perfection is control.
Excellence is spontaneous.
Perfection is judgment.
Excellence is accepting.
Perfection is taking.
Excellence is giving.
Perfection is doubt.
Excellence is confidence.
Perfection is pressure.
Excellence is natural.
Perfection is the destination.
Excellence is the journey. (Anonymous)

One reason so many of us compulsively pursue perfection is that we don't understand what God expects of us. We read Jesus' words in Matthew 5:48 (NIV), "Be perfect, therefore, as your heavenly Father is perfect," and we wonder if God is the ultimate taskmaster. But when the Bible uses the word *perfect,* it usually means "complete," not "flawless."

The Bible says that "Noah was a just man, perfect in his generations. Noah walked with God" (Gen. 6:9 NKJV). My *Strong's Concordance* translates *perfect* in this passage as "complete, full, undefiled, upright, full of integrity and truth." In Genesis 17:1 (KJV), God talked to Abram: "And when Abram was ninety years old and nine, the LORD appeared to Abram, and said unto him, I am the Almighty God; walk before me, and be thou perfect." *Perfect* has the same meaning for Abram as it did for Noah. In Psalm 37:37 (KJV) are these words: "Mark the perfect man, and behold the upright: for the end of that man is peace." *Perfect* in this passage means "complete, pious, gentle, and dear." And where Jesus told us in Matthew to be perfect like our Father, He meant for us to be complete, full grown, and mature.

When I consider my definition of *perfection* during my compulsive days, I realize I was striving to do all things well in order to be considered competent and responsible. It is so refreshing to me now not to have to be perfect as the world defines *perfection*. It's reassuring to me to know that only Jesus Christ was a perfect human being. And because He made the perfect sacrifice for me, I can become perfect (complete) in Him. I have nothing to prove.

Next time you get down on yourself because you can't do all things perfectly, don't beat yourself up. Don't blame other people. Don't keep striving for the impossible. Realize that perfectionism is a sickness; Jesus is the Redeemer. Look to the Source of your strength. You will never be able to be everything you should be. Only Jesus can supply that kind of completeness. Rest in Him.

### Prayer

*Oh, God, how wonderful it is to know that I don't have to be perfect. What a relief to know that You understand my human inadequacies and are ready, willing, and able to bear them for me! When I look to You alone for my completeness, the pressure is lightened, the stress is decreased, the tasks are made easier. Thank You for being a God of mercy, grace, and strength in my weakness. Amen.*

## God's Word to You

And he said unto me. My grace is sufficient for thee: for my strength is made perfect in weakness. (2 Cor. 12:9 KJV)

---

## Affirmation

When I cannot meet the world's standards, I rest in the knowledge that God's standard is completeness in Him.

# Victims or Victors?

## God Promises to Forgive Us as We Forgive Others

⸻

$\mathcal{O}$ne of the hardest demands God makes of His children is the one that calls us to love our enemies—to forgive people who have knowingly and willfully violated us physically, emotionally, or spiritually. When we are hurt by the infidelity of a spouse, abuse from a loved one, vicious gossip, unfair treatment at work, crime, or humiliation, the wound goes deep. Anything that threatens our security, safety, integrity, intelligence, or character is difficult to cope with, much less to forgive.

At one time in my life, I really hated some people who had hurt me. God knew that sometimes I really wanted to see them dead. I obsessed about their deeds and daydreamed about what I would do to get even. Yes, I did! Here I was, thinking I was a good Christian woman with tons of hatred and vengeance, wrath and hostility, in my

heart. I believe my unforgiving spirit eventually mani-
fested itself in a two-and-a-half-year bout with a physical
ailment called phlebitis. Having pains and redness in my
left leg and wearing heavy elastic stockings to aid blood
circulation were parts of my daily routine. Medicines my
doctors prescribed weren't helping. Not even the painful
injections I got in my stomach to aid blood coagulation
were helping. I was in the hospital several times, and I
missed a lot of work. Whenever I sat down, I had to ele-
vate my legs to keep a blood clot from forming and possibly killing me. I was a mess!

Thank God for true friends. Orniece Shelby came to
see me and offered a different prescription altogether.
"Thelma," she said, "I really believe you'll get well if you
forgive the people who have hurt you. Whatever it is, let
it go!" To that insulting statement, I made an emphatic,
uncharacteristically harsh reply, telling her where she
could go for saying something like that to me. (I was not
as strong in my Christian walk then as I am now.)

Several weeks passed, and I wasn't getting better.
Orniece came to see me again and told me the same
thing. "Thelma, Baby, I believe you'd get well if you
would just forgive them for what they did to you." That
time I wasn't quite so defensive. My friend had planted a
seed of truth, and the Holy Spirit had begun to water it.

By the third time Orniece urged me to forgive, I had

become convinced that something might indeed be going on inside me, stifling the healing process. I decided to take my friend's prescription, which included reading my Bible and asking God to help me forgive. Notice, I was not to ask to be healed of phlebitis, but to be given a forgiving heart.

Over time I began to submit to God's will for me to forgive. I asked Him to make it convenient for me to see the people I hated and to help me tell them, "I forgive you." One Thursday after my regular weekly laboratory visit where the technician tested my blood for a medication adjustment, I stopped by an automobile parts store. Guess who was there? Yes, the two people who were parties to my betrayal. The two people I hated. I had asked God to make it convenient for me to tell them I forgave them. He did. (Watch what you pray for, you might get it sooner than you think!)

My heart was pumping overtime. My hands began to sweat. My tongue was heavy. I thought about the vow I made to God, and I remembered that it's better to never make a vow than to make one and break it (Eccl. 5:5). My moment of truth had arrived. With fear and trembling, I approached my enemies, told them that I was keenly aware of the things that had happened and how hurt I had been, but I wanted them to know that I forgave them. They were shocked!

When I left their presence, I felt as if the weight of the world had been lifted off my shoulders. I was delighted by my ability to express genuine forgiveness to them after seriously wanting something bad to happen to them. At that moment, I became a victor instead of a victim. God restored the joy of my salvation. I was given back my song of praise. Boy, did I feel different!

When I returned home the following Thursday from my weekly laboratory visit, my doctor called me to report how pleased he was with my progress. He said the tests showed that I had begun to respond favorably to the medication. Tremendous progress continued for the next few weeks until I decided, *No more medicine.* I knew deep in my heart that I was delivered from my grudges and hatred, and I was healed of my dreaded condition. Praise the name of Jesus!

Now please don't misunderstand me. I am not saying that all people who are sick are in that condition because they harbor resentments. But I am saying that hatred and lack of forgiveness will manifest themselves in one way or another. Trying to get even with people who have hurt us drains our energy and diminishes our productivity. Holding on to our hurts will always have a negative effect on our lives.

Sometimes we just don't want to let go of our grudges and heartaches. We want to hold on to them and watch our enemies suffer. We look for opportunities to bring up the past and rub the guilty persons' faces in what they've done. But while we're in the "get back at them" stage, we are constantly rehashing their actions toward us, our reactions toward them, and our hopes for their destruction. Resentment spreads like a cancer, eating away at the soul. It destroys our hopes and relationships. I know. I've been there.

Have you been there? Are you there now? Maybe your lack of forgiveness has caused guilt feelings, over-sensitivity, physical ailments, poor relationships, problems on the job, lack of trust in others, paralyzing fear of the unknown, or something else that hinders your experience of the abundant life Christ promises. If this is true, you can ask God to help you become willing to forgive, and ultimately to speak forgiveness to those who have hurt you.

Jesus told us that if we are unwilling to forgive, we will not be forgiven. Friend, don't miss out on God's precious grace. Allow the Holy Spirit to administer the healing medicine of forgiveness.

# Prayer

*Father, how deeply I appreciate the fact that You are willing to forgive me for every wrong I've ever done. For You, it is a joy to forgive. The beautiful thing about Your forgiveness is that You never rub my nose in my past transgressions. You choose to "remember my sin no more." Please grant me a forgiving heart like Yours. Help me to let go of my grudges and the bitterness of my past so that I can be a victor instead of a victim. The power to forgive is such sweetness in my soul. Amen.*

## God's Word to You

For if you forgive men when they sin against you, your heavenly Father will also forgive you. But if you do not forgive men their sins, your Father will not forgive your sins. (Matt. 6.14–15 NIV)

## Affirmation

Because I am forgiven by God for my transgressions, I forgive my enemies for theirs.

# Praise Is a Two-Way Street

## God Promises to Delight in Us When We Praise Him

I've always enjoyed praising God in song. Singing praise and worship songs has calmed me when I'm upset, adjusted my attitude when it gets out of whack, given me patience when I'm restless, and infused me with the sheer pleasure of making music to the Lord. I love to sing!

For years, the idea of producing a music album was tucked back in the far recesses of my mind. I thought about it now and then, but I assumed that the probability was remote. My children and several friends had suggested I produce an album, but frankly I didn't think my voice was recording quality. I sang in church sometimes, and I was always singing at home. Sometimes I sang at the end of my speaking engagements and occasionally at weddings. That was certainly no reason to get my hopes up about being a recording artist.

One evening in August 1996, I was driving south on Interstate 35 in Dallas, and the thought again occurred to me to cut a music album. *Now what is this, Lord? I can't do that! Besides, I'm in the middle of preparing for my annual Becoming a Woman of Excellence retreat. I don't have time to deal with a music album.* (Sometimes I argue with God.) I put the thought out of my mind and continued with my plans for the upcoming retreat.

A month later the retreat was behind me, and the idea about recording an album jumped into my mind again as I was driving to work one morning. That time the voice within got more specific. The Holy Spirit seemed to direct me: *Cut the album the weekend before Thanksgiving.* God had my attention. *All right, all right! Whatever You say, Sir!* (I ought to know by now that I'll never win when I try to argue with God.) I called my daughter Vikki, and we started planning immediately.

We began putting the pieces together for what we called a Thanksgiving Gala, to be held at St. John Missionary Baptist Church on November 23, 1996. Vikki made all the arrangements with the recording company, worked out stage and set decorations and lighting, music permissions and contracts, musicians and soloists. My office staff busily prepared invitations, news releases, publicity, and every other detail to make the recorded worship program a success, honoring the Lord. My role in the entire project was minimal. I would simply sing, along with other "unknowns" whom we believed had anointed voices and would allow their talents to be used for the glory of God.

The night of the Gala arrived. The audience attendance was good. The stage and the lighting were warm and worshipful. The recording company was skilled and professional. The music was outstanding! People are still talking about the sacredness and quality of the program. The audiocassette *Jesus, We Give Thanks* is comforting people in hospitals and nursing homes, and blessing people in their homes, offices, and cars all over the nation. People are calling and faxing in orders for more and more tapes. Some people have ordered twenty at a time![1]

I cringe when I think what a major ministry opportunity I would have missed had I continued to ignore the Lord's prompting to produce an album. God had a definite plan in mind: He wanted me to help His people praise Him. He has put the desire to worship deep within our hearts, and He wants us to raise our hearts and voices to Him. The word *praise* is recorded in the Bible *216* times (according to *Strong's Concordance of the Bible*); it must be pretty important! Psalm 22:3 says that God inhabits our praise. When we worship, He is in our midst. That's why there is such great pleasure in honoring God with our praise for all He is and does, for His great love for humankind.

In Zephaniah 3, the prophet painted a magnificent picture of this holy love. After God condemned the religious people of the land for their moral decay, His merciful nature shone forth. He promised to gather His true children, the ones who offered Him praise, and sustain them as He destroyed His enemies. He would restore their fortunes before their very eyes and give them back their joy. And God would respond to His people's praise with His own:

> The LORD your God is with you,
>> he is mighty to save.
> He will take great delight in you,
>> he will quiet you with his love,
>> he will rejoice over you with singing. (Zeph. 3:17 NIV)

How awesome to know that almighty God rejoices over us when we praise Him!

Consider Psalm 147:1 (NIV):

Praise the LORD.
How good it is to sing praises to our God,
    how pleasant and fitting to praise him!

It is *good* and *pleasant* to praise the Lord: good for Him, pleasant for us. Praise is a two-way street. Hallelujah!

---

## Prayer

*Jesus, we give You thanks. Thank You for being an awesome God who deserves all our praise. You are the Holy One. You are the Precious One. You are the Alpha and Omega, the Master of everything. I love You, Lord. I hold You in highest esteem. How thrilling it is to hear You sing back to me when I lift my voice to You in praise! Amen.*

---

### God's Word to You

Let everything that has breath praise the LORD. (Ps. 150:6 NKJV)

---

### Affirmation

When I praise the Lord, He sings back to me with joy.

# *His Eye Is on the Sparrow*

## God Promises to Watch Over Us

$M$y daughter Vikki was independent, adventurous, and courageous as a twenty-something young lady, and she had always wanted to see the world. She set out on an eighteen country tour, and the first six months of her voyage from Dallas to Europe, Asia, and India went well. The next stop was to be Egypt, but God intervened.

She called me from an airport in India and said, "I'm not going on to Egypt as I'd planned. Something's telling me I need to leave and go to Germany. I'll call you in a few days when I get there."

Little did she know that the day after her departure, the day she was scheduled to be in Egypt, war broke out. Operation Desert Storm had begun. Had she gone to Egypt or remained in that area of the world, the possibility of her getting trapped there by the military is frightening to think about. Many Americans were caught there and were not permitted to leave for a number of days.

My son, George, lived in California for a short time. He was not accustomed to or familiar with gang activity. His knowledge of the gangs was limited to what he'd seen on television. But he learned quickly after living in the Los Angeles area for about a week.

One day he wore the wrong color shirt. George, an unsuspecting, happy-go-lucky young man, was leisurely walking to his friend Daryl's house. Daryl was watching out his window and realized the danger George was in. Daryl yelled to George to hurry and get in the house before he was seen. Praise God, George listened. Just as he ran into the house, a car full of gang members drove by the house making loud, frightening threats.

George had another "scared stiff" experience while in California. He'd finished working at Sears that day, and on his way home he noticed a man who looked safe for him to speak to. Remember, George is from Texas. We speak to people whether we know them or not. George greeted the man with his usual friendliness, expecting a nod or verbal greeting in response. George got more than he bargained for. The man pulled out a gun, used profane invectives, said he was waiting for someone to kill that day, and George was the one.

Some people happened to be coming toward them, and George had gotten enough distance between him and the gunman to start running toward the people for protection. The crazy gunman turned away from George and went in the opposite direction. Whatever the gunman's rationale was for not following through on his murderous urge, I believe God showed up again and spared George's life one more time.

In every situation, whether ordinary or life threatening, God assures us that He keeps His eye on us and knows the number of hairs on our heads. Absolutely everything that can happen to us—good, bad, or indifferent—God knows and cares about. God is concerned about us all the time, in every area of our lives, even if nobody else is. He promises that we are never away from His presence.

Does that mean nothing bad will ever happen to us? No. But it does mean that we can have inner peace in this dangerous world. Jesus declared, "I have told you these things, so that in me you may have peace. In this world you will have trouble. But take heart! I have overcome the world" (John 16:33 NIV).

God has promised to watch over His dominion children. Every trial, tribulation, question mark, perplexity, decision, burden, disappointment, heartache, calamity, tragedy, turmoil, loss, danger, exclusion, accusation, threat, or act of the devil is within the scope of God's knowledge and care. He is sovereign, and He knows the outcome of whatever befalls us. He has already worked it out. His ministering angels protect us. His precious blood covers us. His grace and mercy go before us. He has told us,

> When you pass through the waters,
>     I will be with you;
> and when you pass through the rivers,
>     they will not sweep over you.
> When you walk through the fire,
>     you will not be burned;
>     the flames will not set you ablaze.
> For I am the LORD, your God,
>     the Holy One of Israel, your Savior. (Isa. 43:2–3 NIV)

With that kind of assurance, I can sing the words of this hymn with confidence and faith:

> I trust in God wherever I may be,
> Upon the land or on the rolling sea,
> For, come what may,
> From day to day,
> My heav'nly Father watches over me.

I trust in God, I know he cares for me
On mountain bleak or on the stormy sea;
Tho' billows roll,
He keeps my soul.
My heav'nly Father watches over me.[1]

## Prayer

*How consoling it is, Lord, to know without a doubt that everywhere I go, You are there watching over me. Thank You that You are omniscient, omnipresent, and omnipotent. Thank You that You are not limited by time, space, gravity, or atmosphere. Thank You that You prove Your nearness in my most scary experiences. And thank You that no matter what I encounter in this world, You have already overcome it. Amen.*

## God's Word to You

Are not two sparrows sold for a penny? Yet not one of them will fall to the ground apart from the will of your Father. And even the very hairs of your head are all numbered. So don't be afraid; you are worth more than many sparrows. (Matt. 10:29–31 NIV)

### Affirmation

No matter what circumstances I face in this world, I have no reason to fear because God is watching over me.

# Our God Reigns!

## God Promises to Reveal His Truth to All People

The daughter of one of my good friends called me recently and asked me to speak for an annual religious conference. She was Muslim. I reminded her that I am a Christian. She replied that she knew I was a Christian, but her mother and sister in law had told her I was an excellent speaker and that they (the women of Islam) should ask me to speak at their women's conference. I explained to her that Jesus Christ is Lord of my life, and that I talk about Jesus in my speeches. She said, "Oh, just talk about male-female relationships and how you stayed married all these years. We want a mature lady who can be a role model for us in our marriages."

I hesitated before saying yes. As I thought about it, I was reminded of an occasional prayer of mine: "Lord, please give me opportunities to witness for You." And then I was reminded of what He'd told me to do as I was lying on the floor talking to Him in 1995. I'd gotten the impression that He wanted me to accept every speaking invitation as an opportunity to proclaim a word for Him. Jesus told His disciples, "The harvest is plentiful but the workers are few" (Matt. 9:37 NIV). Was I willing to work to gather the harvest? In my spirit, God reminded me that He would be with me. He goes before me, stays beside me, and follows after me. I accepted the invitation.

When the day arrived, there were a lot of women at the New Hope Baptist Church where the conference was held. (I thought it rather strange to hold a Muslim conference inside a Baptist church.) When the time came for me to speak, I began my talk with the greeting, "I greet you in the name of Jehovah, Yahweh, my Creator and my God, and in the name of Jeshua, Jesus Christ, my Lord and Savior." I reasoned that if they can greet assemblies by acknowledging Allah, I could greet them in the name of the Lord. Boy, you could have heard a pin drop. But I had set the stage for who I am in Christ.

I proceeded to talk about my marriage of thirty-six years and how God had brought us out of some of the pitfalls of marriage; how I had to call on Jesus all the time to help me; how the Holy Spirit had guided me with the kind of wisdom I could not possibly have gotten from within myself; how they, too, could have the blessing of this kind of wisdom; how biblical wisdom yields peace and joy; how the joy of the Lord destroys hostility and bitterness between spouses and spills over into the community. Frequently while I was speaking, many of the women shouted out in agreement with what I was saying. There were spurts of applause, and by the end of my speech women were standing up all over the sanctuary happily nodding their heads, waving their handkerchiefs, clapping their hands, saying, "Yes! Speak on, Sister. Tell the truth!" I cannot tell you if they fully accepted the truth that Jesus Christ is the Messiah and Savior of all humankind. I can tell you that they did not reject outright what I was saying. Many of them thanked me for such a powerful message.

Before I went to the conference I'd spent a lot of time in prayer. I asked the Lord to help me speak and act in love and peace. I didn't want to do anything that would negatively affect my Christian witness to those Muslim women. I prayed that God's ministering angels would be there to help me do my Master's will. God heard my prayers and granted abundant grace. My friend tells me that her daughter and other members of Mohammed's Mosque are still talking about how encouraging and enlightening my words were to them. Glory to God!

Now I have a pending invitation to speak for a Jewish conference. I don't know what I'm going to talk about or how I will approach it, but I do know this: wherever God leads me, He will give me the wisdom to represent Him rightly. I also have come to realize that all people are born with an innate desire to be in fellowship with the Creator. The world is looking for God in so many different places. Christians have been given a mandate to go into all the world and preach the gospel to every creature, and I accept that mandate as my own. God gives me opportunities to represent Him, not because I'm so wonderful and know so much, but because I'm willing and available for Him to use me.

Sometimes it feels scary to address people with beliefs so different from my own, but I count it a blessing and privilege to be entrusted with such strategic assignments. I delight in the words of the prophet Isaiah:

How beautiful on the mountains
    are the feet of those who bring good news,
who proclaim peace,
    who bring good tidings,
    who proclaim salvation,
who say to Zion,
    "Your God reigns!" (Isa. 52:7 NIV)

## Prayer

*Father, the whole world is looking for a relationship with You, whether the people know it or not. Some look to various religions, cults, customs, traditions, works, but, praise God, You have provided the Way through Your Son, Jesus Christ. Even when Your Son's name is used in places where it's not popular, people have to take notice that His presence is there. You do reign over every place, person, principality, purpose, and possibility, and You provide a forum for the truth to be revealed. Thank You that Your children can say with confidence, "Our God reigns!" Amen.*

## God's Word to You

The LORD reigns forever,
　　your God, O Zion, for all generations.
Praise the LORD. (Ps. 146:10 NIV)

## Affirmation

I trust God to reveal Himself throughout the universe, and I accept His call to proclaim His good news to all people.

# Notes

## The Thirty-Day Book

1. You may order *Capture Your Audience Through Storytelling* by contacting Kendall/Hunt Publishing Company at P.O. Box 1840, Dubuque, IA 52004-1840, or through the Internet at www.kendallhunt.com. You may also order through Thelma Wells and Associates, 1-800-843-5622.

## The Doctors Had Given Up

1. *The Full Life Study Bible*, 732.

## Praise Is a Two-Way Street

1. Order from Thelma Wells, A Woman of God Ministries, P.O. Box 398020, Dallas, TX 75203; 1-800-843-5622.

## His Eye Is on the Sparrow

1. "My Heavenly Father Watches Over Me," by Charles H. Gabriel. Copyright 1910, renewed 1938. The Rodeheaver Co., owner.

# About the Author

Thelma Wells is an author, speaker, former host of her own television show, retreat sponsor, organizer, executive, wife, mother, grandmother, and active community and church volunteer. She is also president of A Woman of God Ministries and a key speaker at the national "Women of Faith" conferences.

Christian and secular groups often call on Thelma as a speaker and trainer. She has worked with corporations, associations, and educational and governmental institutions, sharing her insights with more than one million people in every state in the U.S. and in numerous foreign countries.

Thelma is the author of several books, including *God Will Make a Way* and *Bumblebees Fly Anyway: Defying the Odds at Work and Home.* She is also a coauthor of *Destiny and Deliverance: Spiritual Insights from the Life of Moses.* She and her husband, George, live in Dallas and have three children and four grandchildren.

Also by Thelma Wells from Thomas Nelson Publishers

# God Will Make a Way

Amazing Affirmations of God's Faithfulness in Everyday Life

When Thelma Wells faced overwhelming hardships and personal loss as a child, her great-grandmother always assured her, "The Lord will make a way somehow." At the age of fifty-five, Thelma began a careful study of God's promises to His people in the Bible. She soon realized her great-grandmother was right: God had been keeping His Word to her for as long as she could remember. In this inspiring and sometimes humorous devotional, Thelma shows how God's promises apply to the challenges you face every day.

**0-7852-7542-8 • Hardcover • 168 pages**